WE'LL GATHER

"WE'LL GATHER LILACS..."

LENNA
BICKERTON

Part Two by her daughter
JUNE HALL

an imprint of
ANNE LOADER
PUBLICATIONS

Dedicated with love to my dear husband, Jim

Florence Lenna Bickerton, 1999

ISBN
1 901253 21 X

Published March 2001

© June Hall
© Vivien Wilson

Typeset and published in Gt Britain by:
Léonie Press
an imprint of
Anne Loader Publications
13 Vale Road, Hartford,
Northwich, Cheshire CW8 1PL
Tel: 01606 75660
Fax: 01606 77609
e-mail: anne@aloaderpubs.u-net.com
Webesite: www.leoniepress.com
www.sleepydogdreams.com

Printed by:
Anne Loader Publications

The author

Lenna Bickerton
*A "farewell" picture taken in France in the
summer of 1999*

Contents

List of photographs

FAMILY TREE

Joseph Bickerton = Sarah Ann (Dean)

James Cloudsdale = Edith (Hitchen)

Eva   Bertha   Douglas

JAMES (JIM)
1910-1996

Edith

LENNA
1915-1999

=

June = David HALL
1938-   1940-1990

Vivien = 1. Ray O'Brien 1947-70
1947-   2. Peter WILSON 1948-

Lorna = Andrew
       McKenzie

Jamie = Anne

Stuart
+ Tonje

Jostein

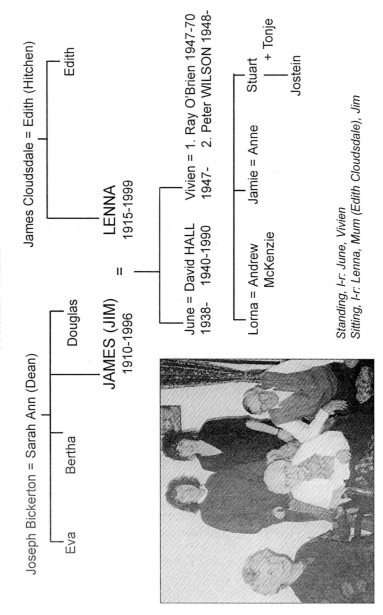

Standing, l-r: June, Vivien
Sitting, l-r: Lenna, Mum (Edith Cloudsdale), Jim

Part One
by Lenna Bickerton

Still life in oils painted by Lenna when she started to attend art classes in her retirement. As a teenager she had been destined for art college until her father lost his job and the 'nest-egg' to fund her studies had to be used by her parents to start a greengrocery business.

Chapter One

Dad came home early one morning, having finished
the night shift, and told Mother that he had been
given the sack. To say she was upset was an understatement: she was devastated, especially after the
whole sorry story was explained.

*O*ur dinner hour was never the same once Tony became part of the family. At that time we did not know what lay in store for us...

But I find my thoughts running on too quickly, so I will return to where I left off in my last book of memories.

I was fourteen years old in 1929 when I left school. There were few jobs that offered a promising career for young people. There was the usual office and shop work, of course, if you were good at arithmetic (which I was not), the sewing factory (and I loathed sewing) or the cake and biscuit factory at Gadbrook. There you were paid a pittance in exchange for plenty of hard work. I hasten to add that as the years went by it was developed into a profitable business by the Broadhurst family and became a good place at which to work. This then was the prospect facing me when I left school.

Dad had a good shift job at ICI, the chemical manufacturers, and due to my mother's careful management they were able to put savings aside "for a rainy day". After much thought and advice from my headmaster, my parents decided to use some of these savings to send me to art school in the hope that I could make a career for myself.

Shortly after this had been agreed, my mother went on one of her usual shopping expeditions to town, which included a visit to the open-air market on Crum Hill. Why the place was named Crum Hill I have never been able to find out: it was a cobbled open space which rose up slightly from Crown Street, levelling out eventually and continuing past the gas works, whose acrid smell permeated the atmosphere. Bargains were to be had amongst the goods which were displayed on the open space or spread out on the ground if no stall was available.

On this particular day there was a gypsy woman telling fortunes and on impulse my mother did something which was quite out of character for her. She entered the small booth where the gypsy sat waiting for clients, gave her sixpence and had her fortune told. Arriving home, she told us that the woman had predicted a change was coming in my mother's life and that this change would be considerable. Even so, she was sceptical about the prophecy, took it "with a grain of salt" and dismissed it from her mind. She recalled the words with some misgivings a few months later, saying "they were the truest words ever spoken."

Now we come to the crux of the matter which is central to the story of my life.

At this time Dad still had his good job at ICI and one day followed another in the same pattern. There was nothing to upset the equilibrium of our lives – or so we thought – but fate had other ideas.

Dad came home early one morning, having finished the night shift, and told Mother that he had been given the sack. To say she was upset was an understatement: she was devastated, especially after the whole sorry story was explained.

It began when a newcomer joined Dad's gang in the drum plant. I believe he was Australian and the type who "knew it all." The men took a dislike to him. When they had their break at around midnight, conversing with one another, this chap always appeared to be contradictory and was prone to boasting – in fact, he got "under their skin", as the saying goes.

One night the men were swapping tales about the "Marbury Lady", a ghost who was said to haunt Marbury Hall, a country mansion in the Northwich district. From time to time she was also seen walking in Marbury Hollows, a local beauty spot, according to various accounts. Over the years sightings were reported periodically by people who swore that they had seen "her". The mystery and legend attached to this poor lady continued as it had done for decades. As children we loved to repeat and embellish these stories ourselves and enjoyed scaring one another. Telling ghost stories was a popular pastime of ours.

I believe that the Barrymore family owned Marbury Hall and its estate in the 18th century and their descendants were still owners well into the 20th century.

To get back to Dad's account of the situation, the newcomer reckoned that he was afraid of nothing, ghosts included. The gang found this too much of a challenge and decided to play a practical joke on him. Some days later, around midnight, out of the blackness of the night a white apparition appeared slowly moving towards the man who was "afraid of nothing." On encountering this vision, he dropped the tin containing his bagging and took to his heels, running up a narrow railway cutting. The gang fell about laughing at the success of their little joke, which soon backfired when they found out that their victim had reported them to the manager. It came to light later that in his flight the man had fallen headlong, cutting his knees, and had been asked to account for his injuries.

Dad admitted that he had been the ringleader and worn the white sheet, but when the manager demanded to know the names of the others involved he refused to tell on them – and was sacked. He always had a streak of devilment in his nature and an aversion to authority at times but, according to my granddad, who always had a maxim ready for any occasion, "workers will be workers and mesters will be bosses…"

My parents went through a very rough patch indeed after this event, as you can well imagine. Dad never dreamt that such misfortune would be the outcome of a foolish prank, and of course was full of regret. He looked around for work for a while, unsuccessfully, then after talking things over with my mother decided to take the plunge and sink their savings into setting up a greengrocery business. At first Mother was loath to agree to this plan. Ever the cautious one she pointed out to him that there were already two greengrocers working in the area. But nothing daunted, the more he thought about it the more he liked the idea of being his own boss, and couldn't wait to put the scheme into practice.

The first problem that confronted Dad was to buy a horse. He knew very little about horses but found a dealer and acquired one, along with a cart. He bought his fruit and veg-etables from Kershaws, the local wholesalers in Northwich. Mr. Wright, whom we called a "gentleman farmer" in those days and was a councillor for our parish of Rudheath, gave Dad the use of a stable on Grange Farm for the horse and later on a small meadow for it to graze in.

Now Dad was set up to start a new way of life.

On the first day, my mother and I watched him move off up the road with "Tommy" pulling the loaded cart, and as we stood there it became obvious that the animal was finding it hard going. Mother turned to me and said: "Your dad's bought a pig in a poke." and tears filled her eyes. Poor Mother, it was all too much for her – it seemed such a precarious undertaking.

Very soon Dad returned Tommy to the dealer accompanied by my Uncle Arthur who had worked for a horse-dealer in his youth – what he didn't know about horses wasn't worth know-ing. If Dad had taken him in the first place it would have saved a lot of anxiety all round. However, luckily, he was able to get his money back and so began the process of choosing another horse, but with an experienced eye to help him this time. Uncle Arthur examined a white pony that Dad quite liked the look of and, apart from finding a small scar on one of his legs, decid-ed that the animal was strong and lively and would be a good worker. He was brought home and this is when "Tony" came into our lives, where he remained for several years.

I mentioned at the beginning that we never had an undis-turbed dinner-hour once Tony stood outside our front gate. Someone had always to be on the lookout because after being fed he was inclined to start walking off, pulling the cart behind him. Patience was not one of his virtues, and he could also be hyper-sensitive to what was going on around him, as we shall see later. Having said this, we realised he was very dependable regarding the work he had to do.

My young sister Edith was allocated the task of brushing up the food that he scattered about, so that everywhere was neat and tidy after Dad had started back on his round.

When my father was trying to establish a round for himself he would call on Rudheath first and then trot off to the next village of Lostock Green, to find new customers. On the way home he took vegetables and fruit to my grandmother's, where there would be a cup of tea awaiting him. Auntie Alice, who lived at Granny's with her family, always gave Tony crusts of bread which he gobbled up. This became a habit but on one occasion when Auntie Alice wasn't there to greet him, he thought that he would jog her memory by walking up the kerb to the front door, which was open, dragging the cart behind him, creating a jangling din with his harness and scraping the wheels on the flags. The family were soon out of the door with crusts to appease his feelings.

When Dad first started in business it came to his notice that one of the other greengrocers threatened "to have him off the road within a week". This was like a red rag to a bull – all it achieved was to make Dad more determined to succeed and he did. More houses were being built in and around Rudheath so there was quite a large area to cover as time went by. Mind you – there were trials and troubles to be overcome in the intervening years.

Up to this time Dad had had a nice garden. He had always enjoyed working in it during his spare time and was very proud of it. Some of the plants we had were seen in lots of gardens in those days, but they seem less popular now. There was mignonette, which didn't look spectacular or anything special, but it had the most lovely scent. Then there was a bushy green plant called "old man", which obviously wasn't its correct name, that also had a sweet smell. There were always lots of nasturtiums, Canterbury bells and lupins. He also kept a few hens and one big white rooster down at the bottom of the back garden. We all went in and out of the hen run to collect the eggs at various times and the rooster always kept a hostile eye on us. One day my sister was left behind after Mum had collected the eggs and when my mother next looked out she saw the cockerel attacking Edith, who was trying to cover her face and head and ward it off. Luckily Dad was at home. He heard Mother shout and he raced down the garden and into the pen to extricate poor little Edith from the nasty situation. He was so incensed that he swore to wring the rooster's neck – and later did.

Now all our way of life was altered. Dad had no time for gardening and such pastimes for all his energy and interest were directed at making a living and creating a good business for the future.

For me, all thought of a career in art was now abandoned and it was imperative to get a job as soon as possible.

Chapter Two

On one occasion when I was working overtime at
Broadhurt's factory at Gadbrook there was a
thunderstorm. Lightning flashed across the large
bare windows, lighting up the stacks of bright new
biscuit tins. My grandmother and mother were both
terrified of thunderstorms and had passed
this phobia on to me.

Round about this time, Dad's younger sister Gladys had started work in Altrincham for the firm of Bannerman's, who owned a sewing factory which made men's shirts and pyjamas and women's clothing. Gladys said that they were taking on young girls to train as sewing machinists. Of all the places for me to seek employment, that should have been the last, considering what I've already mentioned about loathing sewing. However, I went along to the factory, was taken on and was set to work sewing binding on women's pinafores.

As I went into the factory the noise from the machines was deafening. I remember feeling quite nervous but there were two young women who took me under their wing and were most kind and helpful. I remember the name of one after all these years – she was Ella Unwin.

The bindings I sewed around the pinafores were not exactly straight at first but I kept trying. I lasted at the factory for just a week, but I left – not for the reason you may suppose – but because the return train fare between Northwich and Altrincham gobbled up almost all of my wages.

In the end I started work at Broadhurst's biscuit factory at Gadbrook. This was not what I had envisaged for my future life – nor, of course, had my parents – but "needs must when the devil drives", as Granddad would have said. I joined a band of local girls around the ages of fourteen, fifteen and sixteen to-ing and fro-ing every day from eight o'clock in the morning until six in the evening. For this my wage was eight shillings per week with a penny deduction for the hospital fund.

The hours were long for young girls, and the work was arduous. The firm was only in its infancy at this time and the conditions we worked in left a lot to be desired. I had various jobs for a while, first in the Creaming Room, as it was known, using a creaming bag and putting two biscuits together, passing them along to another girl who packed a large tray with them.

There were about twelve of us and we soon got nifty at this and worked quite speedily – that is when the chargehand's beady eyes were on us, which was most of the time.

Later on I was put out to work in the factory proper, "feeding" a large biscuit machine with steel trays. They were not light, I can tell you, and were about two feet square. The biscuits were stamped with the design required and passed on to a conveyor belt which brought them down on to the trays which I had fed into the machine. When the machine was speeded up it would be too bad if you missed a tray and the biscuits would soon be on the floor. A man was waiting to take the trays from me and to place them in the big long biscuit oven, which worked on the same system of conveyor belts.

Small incidents remain in one's mind after almost a lifetime. I remember that there would be very large empty tubs just outside the creaming room doors, which were left open for fresh air. In the summer these attracted hordes of wasps. The thin scrapings of jam that still remained inside the tubs acted like a magnet to them. I was getting on with my work one day, head bent, when I felt a horrible needle stabbing the back of my neck. Of course, I had been stung. It always seems worse when one is attacked unawares.

There were many and varied jobs at the biscuit factory and it was a matter of luck where you were put to work. Some girls went into the bakehouse in the other half of the factory, and that is where one of my school pals, Mary, was. Being 18 months older, she had started at Broadhurst's before me. She helped to weigh out the ingredients required for cakes, fruit loaves, Chorley cakes and all sorts of confectionery. She remembers when she was first sent into the factory as a schoolleaver and was set to work removing cakes from a rack where they had been cooling. Her orders were to tap the side of the tins so that the cakes would fall out on to the table. In her ardour she used more vigour than was necessary and all the nuts were sent flying from the first cake, leaving it bare. Of course at that moment Mr. Harry (Broadhurst) appeared and she was rebuked for her carelessness. We were in awe of authority, coming straight from school, and sharp words from the boss were taken very seriously.

We are both in our eighties now and still meet occasionally. When we do it gives us amusement and much pleasure to recall the old days when we were young. We had a lot to laugh about but we still remember how put out we were when we were admonished for some wrongdoing or other. With the poor wages, long hours and very little entertainment, one would wonder how young folk could have found much to be happy about but in our own way we were content. The pace of life was much slower then, with less rushing about and less hassle, with no computers and other supposedly labour-saving devices. We were not so independent as today's youngsters and in consequence I think we were we were closer to our parents and valued our home life more.

When several of us worked overtime until eight o'clock at night, we were usually put to work on yet another conveyor machine packing biscuits into large tins which were piled up and left until morning for other girls to label. This work was quite enjoyable.

On one occasion when I was working overtime there was a thunderstorm. Lightning flashed across the large bare windows, lighting up the stacks of bright new biscuit tins. My grandmother and mother were both terrified of thunderstorms and had passed this phobia on to me. I remembered how my grandmother would hide, clammy with sweat, in the broom cupboard during a storm, with me as a small child held close to her in the inky blackness.

I was horror-struck as time passed and still the storm raged – and is so often the case when one wants the time to go slowly, the hands of the clock seemed to move very quickly towards 8pm. I couldn't stay in the factory and I dreaded going out in the storm but I had no choice but to dash out with the other girls into the pouring rain. Rudheath was quite a rural village in those days. There was Grange Farm belonging to Mr. Wright with the huge elm trees nearby, a large cottage with a tiny thatched cottage next door, and across the narrow lane two or three farm labourers' cottages. After that it was all open fields. Each time we came past a telegraph pole I could hear one of the girls screech out – which unnerved me still more – and then blue forked lightning would zip across the sky. When I arrived home I just dashed into the house soaked to the skin and collapsed on to the stairs. If I had been running in the Olympics I would have come first and been presented with a medal. My mother, of course, understood my distress.

From that night on I prayed I would never be caught in a thunderstorm again.

Dorothy, another of my biscuit factory friends, was from Winnington. I envied her because she had a bicycle. It was not very long since I had left school and I was immature in some respects, still longing for a bicycle of my own. Seeing that my fervent wish never materialised, I would pester anyone that I knew to let me have a ride on theirs.

I suffered a humiliating experience one day when Dorothy loaned me her bike. We had an hour in which to hurry home, eat our dinner and get back to work – which was quite a distance for most of us. I was late on this particular day and my friend allowed me to use her machine. I remember feeling free as a bird as I pedalled along the lane but when I came to East Avenue I must have been going too fast and consequently lost control. Instead of turning sedately into the Avenue I shot across the road and into someone's front garden. It all happened so quickly but although I had been dislodged from the seat somehow I had managed to cling to the handlebars, so I was dragged along the road, through a small hedge and into the garden. When I picked myself up I found that the front wheel was buckled and – horror of horrors – I had lost both of my shoe heels. Imagine the humiliation I felt as I hobbled along. It seemed an eternity before I came to our house.

My mother was waiting impatiently to give me my dinner so that she could continue with her washing. When she saw what had happened her wrath poured down on me and, worse still, I was ordered to go back and look for the heels. When I returned to the scene of my accident wearing a pair of my mother's shoes, I poked about half-heartedly in the grass, praying that the owner would not rush out to see what I was doing in her garden. However, all was silent, but I never found the heels. I pictured the people at that house when they came to cut the lawn, finding them and being amazed – wondering how they came to be there. Dad was very good at mending our shoes and if I had found the things he could have repaired mine – it would have saved quite a bit of money.

I did not have much time left in which to eat my dinner before I was back off to work. I found Dorothy as soon as I could and related to her what had happened. To my relief, she was very good about it and was even allowed to take her damaged bike to the big garage where the mechanics worked maintaining the vans. They soon repaired the wheel and Dorothy was able to cycle home that evening.

After this debacle I never borrowed anyone's bike again…

When I was sixteen, the Broadhurst brothers invited all their employees to a ball at Parr Hall in Warrington. The talk among the girls was all about what dresses they would wear. My mother agreed to let me go, and then began the search for material for the dress. There was no chance that I would be able to buy one from a shop.

She bought some silky blue material and a few yards of tulle in the same azure shade from the market, and a neighbour made me a pretty ankle length dress from it. With my very dark brown hair and by now a slim figure, I was pleased with the result. What I wasn't so pleased with was the fact that during the few days preceding the ball I had my usual monthly period. Now even in the early 'thirties, there were certain things which you did not do during this time. Myths abounded. For instance if you washed your hair it would be harmful to you. We, as young girls, had no idea what that harm would be – the threat was just so airy-fairy – and yet we believed it to be true. Therefore, instead of washing my hair my mother sprinkled a dry shampoo (a popular commodity from the chemist's) all over my hair. According to the directions on the packet it was then to be brushed in, thus saving the hair from being soaked with water yet cleansing it at the same time. I think that my mother must have been too liberal with this powder, because even after lots of brushing my hair had the appearance of being grey. The following day, the day of the ball, I brushed it madly and felt as though I would have no hair left. I thought I had overdone it, but eventually it began to look normal and by evening all was well. No more dry shampoos for me.

Off I went to the dance with the other girls to Parr Hall, feeling full of excitement. To see everybody in their finery and experience the atmosphere of the special occasion fulfilled all my girlish expectations, especially when one of the bosses asked me for a dance. It was the one and only time that I went to this event, but I always remember it.

As time went by and Broadhurst's biscuits were selling well, they built another factory especially for this product, leaving the old factory for cake-making. There was a lovely view of green fields from the windows but the factory had a corrugated roof and concrete floors and the first winter we worked in it, most of us had chilblains. When summer came we were so hot that we were given a ten-minute break – which had never been heard of before. Most people experienced the discomfort of perspiration soaking through their overalls – so our on break we were out of the building and into the fresh air in a flash.

By now I had a different job to do, brushing the flour which had been scattered on to the uncooked biscuits as they came along the conveyor belt and were stamped by a large and heavy piece of machinery. This belt enabled the biscuits to make a smooth passage down to the steel trays and so into the big ovens. It was quite a light job for me, though I often looked a bit like a snowman. There was no way of controlling the flour which rose into the air – it seemed to be everywhere. I have often thought since that it cannot have been good for us to have inhaled all that dust.

While I was bringing home my meagre wages, which went straight into the housekeeping, Dad was working all hours to make his business a success. Eventually he had extra bonuses twice a year. First of all, he was approached by the Hospital Saturday Committee which organised an excellent fete each summer for Rudheath and district, asking if he would drive the "King and Queen" of the carnival in the procession, using our horse Tony to draw them along in an old landau which belonged to Mr. Wright and was housed in one of his barns at the farm. There would be a sum of money, of course, for his trouble, said the committee, and so Dad accepted. This went on for several years and the crowd who attended the fete would come to watch the King and Queen of Carnival capering and "acting the goat", dressed in outlandish clothes, wearing bright red wigs and waving bunches of rhubarb about instead of bouquets. I always thought that as much as anything else they really came to watch Tony with his high spirits, causing a commotion, until the ever-faithful Uncle Arthur arrived to take over the reins and control. We have a snap of Tony with a garland of paper flowers fastened above his head, which I keep among my souvenirs.

Once, when we were helping Mum to clean the landau – there being lots of straw and dust clinging to it – we found what we thought was a silver cigarette case pushed down one side of the seats. We thought we'd found something really valuable, but it turned out to be only electro-plated.

I took part in the procession on one occasion just after leaving school. I was Britannia and of course my partner was John Bull. His suit was exactly correct, his parents having hired it, but mine was made by my mother from yards of white muslin. The helmet and shield were made and painted by my ever-versatile Uncle Arthur. Someone took a photo of the pair of us and later when the film was developed my mother detected with her usual sharp eyes that the cushion she had pushed behind John Bull's waistcoat to create a bulky appearance had slipped down significantly, so that her original intention was rather "misplaced".

The other contract came from Bratt and Evans, a high class store in the town selling dresses, furnishings and so on, which is still in business – in fact it has become much larger and the shop has been extended. The proprietor asked Dad if he would be willing to meet Father Christmas with the useful landau (provided, of course, that Mr. Wright would loan it, again) at Northwich Railway Station and bring him back to the store. This set us picturing Dad with Father Christmas riding in a stately fashion along Witton Street with the mothers and children waving delightedly at the spectacle. So Dad had a job to do at different ends of the scale, one taking place in June and the other in December.

By now Dad had got used to handling Tony and things had settled down on the whole except for two or three escapades which, I have to say, were fraught with danger.

Meanwhile, and out of the blue, a message came for Dad from ICI asking him to go and see Mr. Spruce, an employment officer. Dad made arrangements for his brother-in-law Tom to help Mother with the business for a short while, then we went to Winnington to find out more. Dad knew Mr. Spruce and said he was "a decent bloke". When asked if he would accept a job in the same department as before, Dad explained that he had started up his own business, whereat the employment officer, after chatting about the situation, advised him to stick to it and continue to make a success of his enterprise, wished him luck and shook hands with him. Dad returned home feeling that a right decision had been made. It had been a morale-booster for him and his will to succeed had been reinforced.

Chapter Three

The cinema to which my sister and I were taken by our parents as children on most Saturday nights was The Central, in Northwich town centre. It was always packed full and a haze of cigarette smoke hung over everybody which persisted until the lights went down and the film started.

*T*here was a set pattern to our lives in our early teens. We worked hard all through the week and met up at the weekend to chat and basically pass the time walking into town, meeting other young folk and spending a few pence on going to the pictures. Some girls were expected to help their mothers with chores around the house if theirs was a large family with younger brothers and sisters. My sister Edie and I were lucky in as much as there were only the two of us, so unless Mother desperately needed a hand, she preferred to be left to get on with it.

There were four cinemas in Northwich at this time: the Castle Picture House, The Pavilion, The Central and a new one built in Witton Street named The Plaza. The Plaza was the first to change over to the "talkies" and we were all eager to try out this new form of entertainment. On the night that I first went, with my boyfriend Jim, I stood in a long queue patiently waiting to be allowed inside, only to be told by the manager that the apparatus had broken down. After his apologies we all dispersed, feeling very disappointed, of course. Eventually with experience everything ran smoothly and it was as if the "talkies" had been with us forever. Al Jolson was one of the stars to appear in these films, in "The Jazz Singer".

I must give a mention to the three older cinemas. The Castle Picture House was situated at the bottom of Castle Hill and seemed to be rather posh in its early days. The girls who came around selling ice cream and nougat were dressed like the waitresses in Lyons' Corner Cafés of that era. They wore little black dresses, tiny frilly white aprons and bandaus round their heads – very smart. There was an added interest at this cinema because during the interval when all the lights went up, the manager Mr. Sherlock – Tom, as he was known – would walk on to the stage wearing evening dress and bow tie and entertain the audience by singing well-known ballads. He had an excellent baritone voice and was much appreciated and applauded. Many years later The Picture House and the next-door mortuary were pulled down to make way for new development in the area. Most of the cinema building which I had thought to be so "posh" when I was young turned out to have been made from corrugated iron, which lay on the ground all around looking most pathetic. So much for girlish romancing.

A little further on, walking over Hayhurst Bridge – a large swing bridge like the Town Bridge that opens up to let large boats with tall masts pass down the river and on to the River Mersey (though there aren't many of those nowadays) – was The Pavilion. This was a cinema which had had a chequered history. When my mother was a young girl before the First World War it was a variety playhouse and the management advertised for a number of pretty girls to be auditioned to be part of a chorus line. It amused my mother when we talked of times gone by to recall the occasion when she, along with a crowd of girls, had turned up for the audition full of excitement. I was pleased to find that she had been one of the "chosen", even though the event had been of temporary duration.

Mother had older sisters who remembered dramas like "Maria Martin and the Red Barn" – a murder mystery – being produced there and other grizzly Victorian-type plays. It was a large black and white building and looked quite old.

The cinema to which my sister and I were taken by our parents as children on most Saturday nights was The Central. It stood at the far end of a short road between some shops in the town centre. The cinema was always packed full and a haze of cigarette smoke hung over everybody which persisted until the lights went down and the film started. Now we know of course how dangerous smoking can be, but years ago people weren't fully aware of this so it was accepted as a matter of course. This was in the time of the silent films with Charlie Chaplin, "Red Indians" and the star pin-ups of the day, Rudolph Valentino, Clive Brooks and so on, who were seen but never heard. A lady would play appropriate music on a piano partly hidden from the audience by a dark green screen. The Central came to a sad end years later when it was burned down.

The last film I ever saw at the Central was around about 1929. It was "Beau Geste" and its star was Ronald Colman. He was world-famous and I thought he was wonderful. He took part in a thriller called "Bulldog Drummond", adapted from a book by Edgar Wallace, which was filmed in the late Twenties. Part of it was shot at Acton Bridge which spans the River Weaver. The hero was supposed to be involved in a car chase with some villains, but if I remember rightly a stunt man took the place of 'my hero' on the bridge.

I was very intrigued with famous film stars – as adolescents usually are – and when my mother bought me a large album one Christmas, I pasted photos in it of my favourites, among whom were Greta Garbo and Douglas Fairbanks Junior.

The Plaza was comparatively modern and like the other picture-houses it was very well patronised. It is now used as a bingo hall – a sign of the times?

A new cinema, The Regal, was built just before the Second World War and is now the only picture-house left in Northwich.

Woolworths built a store in Northwich just before I left school, at the top of what was known as Ship Hill, where an old pub, the Ship Inn, had once stood. It created a lot of interest, being the first branch of "Woolies" we had ever had, and especially as it was announced that none of the goods sold would cost more than sixpence. Not long after this, Woolworths had a neighbour. Marks and Spencers built a new branch of their chain next door.

My first visit to Woolworths came just after I had left school. I had accumulated a shilling in pocket money which was burning a hole in my pocket. It seemed quite empty of shoppers – probably it was on the point of closing for the day. However I was eager to spend my shilling and as I walked on the new floorboards I felt quite conscious of the loud squeak my shoes made. Determined to buy a present for my mother I made my way to a counter that displayed fancy goods. As I said previously, the motto of the store was "nothing over sixpence" and I came away with two wooden candlesticks for my mother, for sixpence each. They were neatly turned and well made; they were certainly worth more than a shilling and she kept them for many years. It wasn't long before the store was doing a roaring trade, being especially crowded on Fridays and Saturdays.

As the days grew shorter and "dark nights" as we called them came around, I went one evening to the pictures with my friend Elsie. When we came out of the cinema it was quite dark and the streets were not as illuminated as they are today. Crowds came surging out of the various cinemas and as usual Witton Street was soon overflowing with people making their way home. Lads were looking out for girls – also as usual. Boys and girls often obstructed the footpaths while chatting to one another, and there would always appear a policeman who would say "Move along there." in a stern voice. On this particular night my friend and I had walked as far as St Wilfrid's R C Church when we met these two boys. At this stage it was known among young folk as "getting off" with girls. They talked to us and asked if they could walk us home. We were hesitant and then walked off, but they accompanied us just the same. As Elsie approached her home I had farther to walk. Little conversation passed between me and my companion. I felt embarrassed more than anything else – and also guilty. I was nearing my fifteenth birthday in a few weeks and I kept wondering what Dad would say if he knew that I was with a boy. I told him to leave me when we reached the top of the avenue, and he asked if he could see me the following Saturday. I said "yes" but I never kept my promise. Later on during the winter I saw the boy again and he once more asked me to meet him. This time I kept my promise because I felt that it had been rotten of me to arrange to see him the first time when I knew full well that I had no intention of doing so. I agreed to see him at the bottom of Station Bridge, which was over a mile from my home. I couldn't relax on my walk for thinking, as I had done before: "What would Dad say if he knew I was out with a boy?" After that meeting I didn't see my dear Jim again until the following summer.

Dad, meanwhile, was working to expand the little business that he had started. As he gained experience he found other sources of fresh vegetables instead of dealing with local business people all the time. However he never lost touch with them completely.

There were times when I was sent to settle his bills, when I was in my early teens. He was always scrupulous about this and never ever owed the Kershaw family a penny, or anyone else for that matter. If it was Thomas Kershaw who I was seeing on Dad's behalf, then he would take the money, give me a receipt and also a shilling for my trouble which I gratefully received. Also there was James Kershaw, a relative of Thomas's, who had a stall in Northwich Market Hall on Fridays. He was a wholesaler in fruit and greengrocery too. If I happened to see flowers on the stall, I could never resist buying a small bunch for my mother but, if he came to serve me, he would never take the coppers I had ready. Mind you, on these occasions it would be getting late in the day.

Fashions changed constantly as they always do, and around about this time there was a passion for things Egyptian. I remember a stall in the market which was displaying hats that were made to look like the headgear of the Sphinx. My mother bought one for me after much cajoling. It was made in a kind of soft fibre which clung to the head. It had stripes of azure blue and silver, and cost two or three shillings. After acquiring the hat I only wore it a few times and took a dislike to it.

Now we come to the other outlet I mentioned. This was

Sandbach Market. Dad would take my mother along and they would trot off with the horse and cart on a Thursday to buy fresh fruit and vegetables. Sandbach was not far away, roughly eight miles from Rudheath and quite a pleasant journey going via Middlewich. It was on such a day as this that they had their first encounter with Tony's "other side". Dad said that they had turned into Croxton Lane and were trotting quietly along when across the fields came the noise of squealing pigs. A farmer was killing the animals and the breeze was bringing the smell of blood with it. When it reached Tony, he bolted. Dad said that he hung on to the reins like grim death and Mother to the cart, with oranges and apples flying in all directions. Eventually, with as much strength as he could muster, he brought Tony to a standstill and between them things were put to rights, while Tony munched the grass under the hedgerow. Looking back in time, it was a blessing that there was no traffic as there is today, and that it was a long quiet lane. After this, the journey was resumed, for Tony had calmed down, and my parents arrived home safely if slightly ruffled.

Long after this escapade there was a second fiasco, this time nearer home in Gadbrook Lane. I forget what scared him on this occasion but thankfully Tony brought himself to a standstill – I believe in the entrance to Wrights' farm where he was stabled. I think he must have recognised that he was near home.

When summer evenings came around my mother, young sister and I would accompany Dad occasionally on his visits to various farms around Lach Dennis, Goostrey and what we used to call Rudheath Woods. There is very little left of these ancient woods now, as clearings have been made over the years and private houses built on the land.

I remember very well one particular farm at which we called – Woodside Farm, it was. It belonged to two bachelor brothers and their spinster sister. They looked quite old to me, the brothers big and tall and the sister tall and gaunt. She wore

old-fashioned clothes – long thick black skirts and black blous-
es. They all wore clogs which clattered on the stone flag floors
as they walked to and fro. One of the brothers had a large
round pale face, like a full moon, I thought. Mother could not
stand him. She said he always tried to "pick a rise" out of people, goodness knows why, probably he thought he was being
clever at someone else's expense. Nevertheless, Dad dealt with
this family for several years, buying eggs and other goods from
them.

On another occasion we went to buy fruit from a farm. Dad
left Tony quietly standing in the cobbled yard while the three
of us went inside the house. After Dad had struck a bargain
with the farmer and bought a large hamper of damsons, he
placed them outside one of the barns and went with the farmer
to look at some potatoes while we sat talking to the farmer's
wife. After about twenty minutes we were ready to leave.
Mum went out first and there was Tony with crimson froth
coming from his mouth. For a split second, she said, she
thought that it was blood and that he had managed to injure
himself. Then she saw him spitting damson stones from out of
the side of his mouth. There were stones all over the ground.
He had crept quietly along until he had found the hamper of
fruit. It was laughable but we hoped he had not been dipping
into the damsons for long. This horse of ours certainly possessed a strong character of his own.

Chapter Four

Jim was of a very quiet disposition but always had a ready smile and this is what endeared him to me most of all, for there were times when he could have been excused if he had looked miserable. Jim had been employed by ICI but had been laid off with thousands of other young men.

*E*very year when Whit Monday came around, a regatta was held on the River Weaver, organised by Northwich Rowing Club. Boat crews competed from many outlying districts and our local Sir John Deane's Grammar School always put up strong opposition. I should say that this event started in the 1800s; it still takes place on Whit Mondays and when I left school it was something to celebrate with crowds of young people walking along the river bank, all very colourful. I don't think there were too many attractions happening around that time, where we could join in an open-air event, except for the fete days.

I went with Flossie, a friend who lived in the same avenue as myself, when we were both fourteen years old. We had called on Flossie's sister-in-law who had recently had a baby and lived at Castle. After admiring the new baby we set off along the river to watch the regatta, each of us wearing a new coat. My coat was of light brown tweed with a half-belt at the back, and Flossie's was green with gauntlet cuffs. I think that I was suffering from puppy-fat at that time and was at my bonniest, but my friend looked quite slim in her new finery. We were very proud of ourselves because new coats didn't come our way that often and when they did they were meant to last quite a while. We couldn't discard them on a whim because they had become a bit unfashionable – not like today's youngsters. Anyway, it was Whitsuntide, which was in itself a very special time of celebration. Nowadays, Whit Sunday comes and goes and very few people seem to notice. There are no Whit Walks or similar events any more.

During the summer months Verdin Park was the place to be for a pleasurable Sunday afternoon or evening. The band would be playing in the attractive wrought iron bandstand in the middle of the park, with the statue of Sir Robert Verdin standing close looking benevolently around. It had been erected in gratitude for his good works for the town. The Victoria Infirmary which we have in the park today began originally by being a sandstone building which he gave to the citizens of Northwich as a hospital and which is now incorporated into a large and very modern complex of hospital, physiotherapy rooms, X-ray department, swimming pool for disabled and arthritic patients, and so on. Sir Robert would be very pleased if he could see it now. He had also provided some brine baths (good for rheumatism.) but owing to a landslip they were thought to be unsafe and new brine baths were built in Victoria Road.

But, to get back to Sundays in the park... I was making my way out of it one Sunday evening after being with some girls from work when a lad I had been at school with saw me and said that he was on his way home too. I was glad of his company, for it was a long walk. We got to the gates when who should come along but Jim with his pal. He looked quite put out and not very pleased as we passed by. He evidently thought that I had made a date with this boy. Joe was only accompanying me on his way to Lostock Green, the next village to Rudheath, but then Jim had tried to start up a friendship with me earlier in the year and it had come to naught.

Amazingly we bumped into one another in the autumn at a fair. This time I stayed with him and we experienced "all the fun of the fair." Girls and boys were riding around on the roundabouts while we went on the swing-boat. When I look back I see these old creaking swings as though they had come out of the ark. It cost only a few coppers to go on them and usually there was a girl sitting on one wooden seat and a young man opposite on the other. Your partner would pull hard on a rope and the boat would start swinging. Of course, the harder he pulled, the higher you would go. Girls would be screeching with excitement. Some boats looked as if they would tip right over, as lads stood up to pull harder on the ropes. I'm sure they weren't all that safe.

This fair was held every September on some waste ground behind The Green Dragon pub in Witton Street. The organ blared out across the fairground and could be heard well into Northwich. There was a Wall of Death, when riders on motorcycles would tear round and round a huge wooden structure going faster and higher until it looked as though they would fly out at the top. Great excitement. There were also the usual coconut shies, hoop-la stalls and hobby horses which went up and down, faster and faster, while the youngsters on them clung to the central brass pole.

Adults as well as young folk would be to-ing and fro-ing along the narrow footpath that led to the fair, and as Jim and I made our way on this occasion down the path, who should come along but my mother and father. I turned round and whispered: "Here's my Mum and Dad." Jim hung behind to let them pass and they just said "Hello", nodded, smiled and walked on. I felt quite relieved.

This was the first encounter of many. We started seeing one another regularly after this and he would meet me out of work at six o'clock. He was of a very quiet disposition but had always a ready smile and this is what endeared him to me most of all, for there were times when he could have been excused if he had looked miserable. This was the 'thirties Depression when millions were out of work. Jim had been employed by ICI but had been laid off with thousands of other young men. He, being optimistic, looked around for other work, hoping to be taken on, even travelling further afield on his bike when there was nothing in this area – only to be told that there was not enough work for their local men. In the event, he was out of work for almost five years. Although he kept his worries from me – or thought that he did – in those lean years, as I got to know him well I could sense the strain and frustration of seeking employment where none existed began to leave its mark. To compound everything else, the Means Test was introduced and the authorities came down hard on anyone who tried to earn a shilling or two to relieve the hardship of those times. At one stage a person sent from the Ministry had the authority to come into a claimant's home to look around and see if there was anything of value there. I was always grateful that Jim had good and caring parents who tried to do their best for him.

In the early part of our friendship I had arranged to meet him one Saturday evening outside the old Pavilion. It had been a very hot summer's day which I had spent with my mother, sister Edith, Auntie Alice and her family at Pickmere beside the lake. We had taken sandwiches with us and bought a pot of tea from an old lady who lived nearby. She would always oblige, lending cups and so on.

When the hot day turned into evening I left the family and set off to walk to Northwich to meet Jim. I had already walked from Rudheath to Lostock with my mother to pick up Auntie Alice and family, and then on to Pickmere. My shoes were made of fabric, with high heels which were fashionable, but the heels were not made of leather but wood – or some such stuff. By the time that I got into Northwich both the shoes and I were feeling the strain. I had got within a hundred yards of The Pavilion, it was going dusk, thank goodness, and people were intent on going about their business, when without warning the heel broke off my shoe. Horror of horrors. I thought, "What is it about heels and me? Why should this happen to me again." But of course the strain of all the previous walking had put paid to the shoes. Jim was waiting for me and as I mingled among the crowd in the dusk things were not too noticeable. We went into the picture house, Jim leading the way to our seats (I made sure that I didn't walk in front of him.). Soon after we took our seats, the National Anthem was played prior to the start of the film. There was a scraping and shuffling of feet, as usual, as we the audience stood to attention.

I remember that it was a Bing Crosby film, one of his early ones, of course, and in it he pushed a pretty girl on a swing. He sang: "I will gather stars out of the blue for you, for you". I got absorbed in the romantic story at the time, forgotten now. And forgotten also was the heel for the time being – remembered with a shock as we stood up and the lights came on. We walked all the way up Roker Park, through Danefields, up Sandbach Hill near Shipbrook and on home. I don't know how I kept up the pretence that nothing was wrong, trying to tiptoe to counteract the heel on the other shoe. Not a word was spoken, then or ever, about it between us. I got embarrassed for next to nothing, let alone this situation. Girls were not as outspoken or confident then as they are today when nothing seems to faze them. Now it would probably just have been a laugh.

When I first visited Jim's family they lived opposite Leftwich Post Office in a terrace of cottages which has now been replaced by council houses. Danebridge School was only a few hundred yards down the road. There was also a confectioner's shop nearby and Miss Postles, who owned it, baked home-made cakes there. Jim told me he delivered them to some of her customers before he went to school in a morning. When we were reminiscing, he said that one day he took his much-loved little puppy with him (unknown to Miss Postles, of course). He was riding a very heavy bicycle with a large iron carrier at the front. The inevitable happened as he rode along. While he was trying to keep hold of the puppy some of the cakes slid off the wooden tray on to the ground. He said they looked all right so he put them back in the tray. Boys.

Miss Postles sold off any cakes left at the end off the day for next to nothing, so "stale cakes" were often requested.

My future father-in-law was a very good crown green bowls player and Jim was even better. His Dad would treat him to a game at the Bowling Green Inn at Leftwich when he finished his shift at ICI in an afternoon. That was something for him to look forward to as both he and his Dad had the same quiet nature and enjoyed one another's company enormously. His other relaxation was going to watch Northwich Vics play on the Drill Field. It only cost a few coppers to watch them play football if you stood on the bank. He would come to our house on a Saturday, after the match, and at first I thought he had a cold, seeing that he was speaking with a croaky voice, only to find after many occasions later that he had been supporting his team in a very serious manner. (He wasn't so quiet then.). He supported the Vics from being a lad, all the years of his life.

As my family got to know Jim and like him, Dad would ask for his help now and again when he was late finishing his round and darkness had fallen. My mother and I were always edgy on these occasions, remembering Tony's highly-strung ways, and yet when November 5th bonfires were lit one year, for some reason which I can't explain, we both sat chatting happily waiting for Dad and Jim to return. And return they did, with Dad being carried in by two men, followed by Jim with his hands raw and bleeding. What a shock it was to us. My young sister was dispatched out into the garden with the sparklers she had been waving about. The doctor was called for and Dad was carried upstairs where he was examined. All had gone well, it appeared, until they turned into School Lane, almost at the end of their journey. At that moment, as they passed School House, a firework was set off with a bang. The outcome was obvious. Tony bolted, throwing Jim off the cart on to some gravel. As Dad fell the back wheels of the cart went over his legs. Although he was in a poor state, nothing was broken, but the legs were badly bruised and swollen, causing him to be laid off for some time. Jim's hands needed attention but between him, my mother and Uncle Tom, business some-how survived until Dad had recovered. Tony, by the way, was unhurt as before. That was the last of his escapades. I don't remember anything untoward happening again – at least noth-ing that could be classed as dangerous.

In 1933 an auction sale was held in Marbury Hall. The gen-try who had owned it had sold it previously to a businessman, but it soon changed hands again and this is when the sale was held. It was never to be the stately home it had once been.

Mum and Dad went along out of curiosity as did crowds of people including, of course, serious buyers. At this time I was at home "on the club" having dropped one of those steel biscuit trays on my big toe. How I longed to go along with them, just to see inside Marbury Hall where the mysterious ghost of the white lady had originated – but rules were very strict then. If you were on the club, you could be reported if you were to be seen enjoying an event like this, even though you might be hobbling along with a stick.

Instead I sat at home gnashing my teeth. Loving history as I did and do, all that I could think of was the fact that I would never be able to see inside this historic place and soak up its atmosphere.

Chapter Five

I was out of a job now but it wouldn't be for long. Girls could get work more easily than men at that time. I went along to the Labour Exchange where there was a small amount of benefit, and looked for work.

CHAPTER FIVE

*L*ater that year I was visiting relatives at Lostock and met up with two girls I had known since childhood. They both worked in service in the Manchester area. It was their afternoon off and they filled my head with all sorts of tales, of how beneficial it was, how you would be able to save quite a bit of your wages, how well paid, how you wouldn't be slogging away in a factory, etc. etc.

All this I inwardly digested and then approached my mother about leaving Broadhursts' and getting a job in service. She didn't think much about the idea, but I contacted those girls again and they helped me to get a place at Eccles outside Manchester. I had visions of saving up money towards the future because I knew that Jim was serious about us getting married if only he could find work. I can understand him being upset at the time but I thought I was being clever, launching out into a different job where I would be better off financially.

Mum and Dad took me to Eccles where the lady of the house greeted me warmly. I was introduced to her two children and her husband, and my parents left for home. I was acquainted with my duties and the family seemed pleased with me, but when I went to bed that night I knew I had made the wrong decision. How ridiculous of me, what a fool I had been listening to those girls. I missed Jim and my thoughts went round and round in my head. I was just like my mother – I was already homesick.

Of course I had to keep my bargain, as long as I could, that is. I got on with my work and nobody knew how I felt. I had been there a few days when I wrote home to my parents and also posted a letter to Jim, telling him I would be home in a fortnight on a day off.

I was in the kitchen washing up two days later when I saw my parents passing the window. They must have read between the lines and had come to take me home. What a fiasco. I was torn between sheer relief and feeling a fool. My employer was justifiably annoyed at being deprived of a reliable worker: she said that the children had "taken to me", and tried to persuade me to remain, but in the end I came away with my parents. I never in my wildest dreams expected to see them turn up at that house, but I certainly realised that service was not for me and that they had done the right thing – apart from the utter embarrassment of the situation.

The first thing that I did when I got home was to go to Jim's house at Leftwich. I knocked on the door and he opened it with a look of amazement when he saw me standing there. The relief was mutual and I said I would never leave him again – and I never did.

I was out of a job now but it wouldn't be for long. Girls could get work more easily than men at that time. I went along to the Labour Exchange where there was a small amount of benefit, and looked for work. In the meantime we went for walks as usual and when we stayed in with the family we would play records on the cabinet gramophone. Mother treasured this as it was a nice piece of furniture as well as being a record player. Just picture this nowadays, as being an instrument of pleasure. The changing of the little steel needles from a small tin box, the constant winding up of the gramophone when it ran down, going slower and slower if you weren't nimble enough to catch it in time, and making the most comical sounds in the process. Apart from the more modern records there were a number of second-hand ones that Dad had bought in a job lot from someone who had sold up their business. They were good too, in condition and content. We had "In a Monastery Garden", various semi-classical pieces and so on. Our favourites were the romantic popular songs of the day, of course. "Little white lies", "The object of my affection", "Hold me honey, won't you hold me" and later "Stormy weather", "Smoke gets in your eyes" etc.

Dad had bought a second-hand car by now. In the first place

he had a three-wheeler which was always difficult to start. It attracted little boys who appeared on the scene from nowhere as soon as they heard the engine spitting noisily. They would revel in puffing and blowing and pushing until it got going. The other car was more reliable – and a four-wheeler, what's more – but I can't remember the make. Dad would take us out on a Sunday sometimes, and we would go as far as the Derbyshire moors. Mum would say: "This will do us good – it will blow the cobwebs off us" and it certainly did as Jim and I wandered off across the moors. We were glad to accept my parents' offer of a "ride out" now and again, otherwise we would have resorted to our usual country walks. We were only young, life was quite humdrum at that period, and Jim longed to find a job to be independent.

While I was unemployed I would go along to the Labour Exchange with a friend from my school days. On the way back, I was always asked into her house to have a cup of tea with her and her mother. They lived in a lovely old farmhouse which had a pear tree in the large front garden. There were barns also where we used to play as children, acting out plays in a home-made theatre with one or two other girls.. This old farmhouse was built along Middlewich Road, which used to be known as Penny's Lane, and was much narrower of course in the olden times. There was a small bakery next door and it always had a delicious smell of fresh bread as you walked into the shop. My mother bought her bread from here and Eric the owner's son would deliver it, sometimes on his old iron bike with a large carrier at the front. The main grocery order would come from the Co-op by horse and cart. I think that the area must have looked very picturesque once. Even when I was a child there were very few houses along that stretch of road. Now the farmhouse has gone and the bakery, and many houses line the road, which is wide and extremely busy with traffic.

My sister Edith had now left school and was seeking employment. Word passed quickly when a job became available and she heard from someone about vacancies at Knutsford Laundry. It was fortuitous that I was free at that time to take her for an interview because Mum was busy behind the scenes helping Dad with the business. Edie got the job and was taken on there and then. It was a lovely summer's day and I was tempted to set off down the country lane to walk home, remembering that when my mother was a very young girl she had walked all the way from Northwich to Knutsford on May Day (with her older sisters) and back home again. This was the only way that they were able to watch the celebrations. After considering the idea, I decided to catch the bus home.

There was a spinster lady who accompanied my sister every morning on the way to Northwich Station, but instead of taking the direct route along Middlewich Road, she would insist on making a detour which took them a bit longer, and they had to rush on the last lap to catch the train. She would tell Edie it was good for their health. There's none as queer as folk.

During the time that my sister was employed at the laundry the work was arduous to say the least. There was one job where large rollers pressed men's shirt collars and the collars would come flying down from these hot steaming machines like fishes, she would tell us – hundreds of them, which were hot to the fingers.

When after working there for quite a time she gave in her notice, the management asked her why she wanted to leave. She said it was like an interrogation, as though she were giving up some wonderful job.

Not long after this I applied for work as a shop assistant at Woolworths and was taken on. I worked on various counters but eventually went with another girl on the children's toys. She lived on Witton Park and we got on very well together. Our Fridays and Saturdays were hectic and the time flew by.

I had an operation during the time I was there, to remove my tonsils. I was nearing my twentieth birthday and I had been plagued with sore throats off and on for years, so my doctor advised an operation as soon as possible. I was only in hospital for a day and a night, but the surgeon who removed them commiserated with me, saying that it was a much more painful experience than having them out as a child. Part of my work on the toy counter had been to blow up all kinds of coloured balloons, but after I had my tonsils removed I was never able to blow up a balloon again.

When Easter was approaching, everything quickened up. We got busier still and I was asked if I would try my hand at writing children's names on the chocolate eggs. Having been introduced to using a creaming bag at Broadhursts' when I first left school, I found it to be easy. At the weekends there would always be a queue of mothers with their children waiting to have their names written in icing on their Easter eggs and I got a "dab hand" at it. I found the girls at Woolworths very pleasant to work with and really enjoyed my time there.

Jim was still out of work and still trying to find a job. About this time there was a retired cabinet maker who lived on Witton Park. He was very concerned about young men who, through no fault of their own, led lives of anxiety with no jobs to look forward to in the foreseeable future. He started up a project whereby he would show any young man who was willing to learn, how to set about making various pieces of furniture. Jim was very willing to try his hand at it and went along to meet this gentleman. He found him to be a very worthy person, and under his tuition made some really attractive pieces of furniture – a wardrobe, a Welsh dresser and a blanket chest for me. Granted the wood was not oak, walnut or anything expensive, but the furniture was strong, very well made and good to look at. I was so proud to possess it and knew that if he had had the chance to serve his time in the joinery trade, Jim would have been excellent at his work. He was a good all-rounder, excelling as a schoolboy at cricket. He was a fast bowler and was chosen to play for Cheshire but he was unable to take this up because of the usual lack of funds. Cricket was an expensive game, what with the white flannels, blazers and all the gear. On leaving school he was good at maths and drawing, and his headmaster had said that draughtsmanship or even architecture was within his scope, but like me, there was not the wherewithal to back him up at that time. Chances did not come often to children of working class parents in the 'twenties and 'thirties.

*Dad (James Cloudsdale), Lenna, Edith and Mum (Edith
Cloudsdale) enjoying a picnic, about 1932*

*The only surviving photograph of Tony the horse. He is on his
best behaviour for Rudheath fete, 1930. Dad and Lenna are
standing by the trap.*

Teenage sisters – Edith and Lenna about 1935

Jim and Lenna, shortly before their wedding in 1937

Lenna with June, their new baby, 1938

Precious moments together in wartime – Lenna, June and Jim, about 1941

Out for a bike ride...

Opposite page and above:
Father and daughters – Jim and June, 1942,
Jim and Vivien at the seaside, 1950

Jim (back right) during the War, with a defused bomb

Lenna loved gathering lilacs on their trips in the countryside

Above: Mother and daughter – Mum and Lenna at Llangollen

Below: Day trip to Llandudno, Vivien, Jim, Lenna and June, 1950

Left: Dad and Mum in the 1950s

Below: Lenna and Jim enjoy their golden wedding celebration in 1988

Right: June and her late husband David at the 1988 golden wedding party (also their own wedding anniversary)

Below: Christmas 1990. Back row: Lenna's grand-children Stuart, Lorna, Jamie; seated: Lenna, Vivien, Jim, Vivien's husband Peter

Chapter Six

It seems almost medieval now when I think about it, that children at Rudheath knew practically nothing about some of the villages further afield unless they had relatives living there, and I'm sure that in the 'twenties that applied to most children wherever they were.

uring this period of my life I found Vale Royal. Jim had always, as a lad, known this area. Along with his school pals it was easy from Leftwich, where he lived, to walk along the River Weaver for a few miles and so enter into Whitegate Park and the realms of Vale Royal Abbey. Actually there had not been a religious order or an abbey there for almost 500 years. A country mansion had been built in its stead. As the years went by, no doubt some of the remaining ruins of the abbey were incorporated into it. Nevertheless although it was a private dwelling and estate at this time, belonging to Lord Delamere, schoolboys were tempted to get a near as possible to it up the long drive. Jim told me that thousands of daffodils grew in front of the Abbey and of course some ended up in the hands of the lads to take home. There was also a large eagle kept in a cage near the house and many pheasants in the grounds. I could just imagine how the boys fled when a gamekeeper appeared, as it seemed they always did, but knowing the ways of lads it wouldn't have been their last incursion into Vale Royal.

Meanwhile in their familiar part of the world these Leftwich lads would arrange football matches from time to time with lads from the village of Moulton, about three miles away. Woe betide them if they won the match though: they would have to be ready to run or most likely they would get stones thrown at them by their opponents. Jim and his pals would take to their heels and dash across the fields down to the river bank and so make their way home along the River Weaver to Leftwich. In spite of this, they still played at Moulton.

They got up to mischief and danger now and again when they were in that area. If they possessed a penny or two they would be drawn as if by a magnet to the railway lines that run over Vale Royal Arches. Making their way up the embankment, they would place their pennies on the line, hide and wait for an express train to thunder past. Afterwards they retrieved their pennies which by then would have been flattened out to twice their normal size. If their parents had realised where they were, I doubt they would have ventured near the Arches again.

It seems almost medieval now when I think about it, that children at Rudheath knew practically nothing about some of the villages further afield unless they had relatives living there, and I'm sure that in the 'twenties that applied to most children wherever they were. Living as we did in Rudheath Park, as it was known then, the areas we traversed were Danefields, "up Rudheath Woods", and Whatcroft with its Hall and estate. We tended to drift in a certain direction, time after time, "traipsing" in small groups with, it seemed, all the time in the world to spare.

But to return to my favourite place – now almost twenty years old as I was, I walked up the river to Magpie Lodge with Jim and entered what I thought of as the magical world of Vale Royal, down into the bluebell wood and on to Rookery Pool with its water-lilies and rhododendrons lining the pool. The impact of it has remained with me always – it was the loveliest place I had ever seen: peaceful, serene, and I thought: "Those monks in the 12th century certainly were clever when it came to choosing a place to live."

It drew us back time and again over the years, even during the war when Jim was a member of the bomb disposal squad attached to the Royal Engineers – a cold-blooded job when called upon. He would come home on leave and we would be surrounded in peace and quiet and feel thankful to be together. There would be two or three men fishing in the pool from a boat, more often than not.

Later we would bring our young daughter June with us and later still our younger daughter Vivien, who was always fascinated by Monkey Lodge, a small cottage among tall trees, which no doubt made it rather gloomy inside, as the spreading beeches leaned above its roof. Now, years later, the huge beech trees that were in close proximity with it have been cut down

Monkey Lodge, Whitegate, from a water colour drawing by Vivien, about 1963

to let in more light, and the stucco on the walls – with its figures of a monkey, a sailing boat and a coat of arms – is plain for all to see. The cottage has been enlarged and it is no longer a mysterious little place in the woods.

The woodland that surrounded Rookery Pool when I was twenty was cut down after the war, but as we drove down Whitegate Lane after an absence of several years, we realised that nature had taken its course and the woodland had rejuvenated itself.

Arthur Chambers, a friend of the Bickerton family, once loaned me a large tome about the history of Vale Royal and the connection of Ida the nun attached to it. Legend or truth? It is also fascinating to realise that the Abbey took decades to be built, depending on the then King Edward I's magnanimity and if there was enough money in the royal coffers to donate towards the work. According to records, he promised to build the most magnificent abbey in the land after his son Edward II, then the first Prince of Wales, was rescued – by the grace of

God – from drowning while crossing the Channel from France. Hence the little boat on the walls of Monkey Lodge. A search was made to find the most lovely and suitable place to build this abbey and eventually (after the monks abandoned nearby ague-ridden Darnall) the land overlooking the River Weaver in Cheshire was chosen and named Vale Royal. It still is to this day a lovely area in spite of modern building going on here and there. It's a great pity that hardly a stone remains of this most beautiful abbey, unlike the ruins of Fountains Abbey and others in North Yorkshire. It would seem that from the very first relations with the inhabitants of Winsford and the surrounding district were anything but peaceful. The Abbots at various times came into conflict with them over taxes, and its history was cut short by the Dissolution of the Monasteries. Even now, in my old age, my imagination is stirred when Vale Royal is mentioned.

Through the long summer days of 1936, Jim would meet me when Woolworths closed on Wednesday afternoons and take me home where his mother would have dinner waiting for me. She was always a very kind person and an excellent dressmaker. Her versatility was put to very good use when hard times came to the family and the children were young. After our meal we would set off up the river, cross over the bridge at Vale Royal locks and enter Whitegate Park by way of Magpie Lodge. Rookery Pool would be very still and mysterious with its lily pads spread out over the water. We had an old Kodak Brownie box camera with which we took various black and white photographs of the scenery. One I remember taking was of two men in a boat quietly fishing. We thought it was funny, for they never realised we were there, let alone taking a snapshot of them – whoever they were. Coming out of the park, opposite Monkey Lodge, we would walk to the end of Whitegate Lane, catch a bus into Northwich and make our way home to Rudheath.

During the 'thirties the desperate anxiety men felt at being out of work, unable to find employment, grew. I know from first-hand experience how badly it affected a man to have no job and no independence. This desperation culminated in men from the North East setting out on the Jarrow March to London to put their petition before the Prime Minister. A branch of the march came through Northwich on its way South. Jim, living in London Road, Leftwich, watched them quietly marching along. He said that housewives hurried out to ply the men with cups of tea to show their affinity with the cause. Eventually the marchers' tired legs took them to what had once been the town workhouse, where they rested for a while. This building was built in 1837, just as Queen Victoria ascended the throne, specifically as a workhouse for people who had reached the end of their tether, with no work and no home. I find it ironic that these men in the 1930s were only too glad to rest their weary bodies in the same place before resuming what turned out to be a fruitless journey. The old workhouse is a fine building, more Georgian than Victorian – after all, it was built just as the Georgian era was coming to an end. The opulent boardroom at one end was built considerably later. Today it houses the Salt Museum, which I think is unique in this country and as such deserves to be cherished.

In 1936, after almost five years on the "dole", Jim was offered two jobs in the same week. Once offer came from ICI and the other from Dutton's Tannery which stood in Dock Lane, off London Road. Always bearing in mind that ICI could make men redundant in their hundreds (as had happened to him originally) when they thought it appropriate, and the fact that it would be a case of "last to come, first to go", Jim chose the job at the tannery. The thought of being out of work again was unbearable to him. If only he could have seen into the future. Alas, none of us can do that.

Dutton's was a caring family business at this time, and

everyone said that although the wages were low you had a job for life. That suited Jim fine. Not having done hard physical work for a long time, it was not easy during those first few weeks at Dutton's. The work involved using iron tongs to draw a number of sheepskins together from the pits where they had been left to remove the wool. They were quite heavy, I should imagine, when they were soaking wet. Jim's hands were raw and sore and had to be attended to until they became hardened and accustomed to the work. However, I never heard a word of complaint pass his lips, for all that it was a hard and gruelling job. He was not a large, hefty person, but his stoicism made up for that.

While he was working at Dutton's, Jim made me squirm by telling me that a man was employed regularly to bring in a cartload of dog dirt from the Cheshire Hunt Kennels at Sandiway which was used in the treatment of the sheepskins. The chap delivered coal to customers during the week – hopefully not in the same cart.

Now that his position was stable, I started to collect things for my "bottom drawer". This, as any young woman of that era would know, was a term for anything that would be useful when setting up home as a bride. My parents would buy me table linen, kitchen utensils, and so on, from time to time, and relatives would also follow suit. If you saw some article you fancied for your future home and could afford to buy, that also would go in the "bottom drawer".

Ambition was not rampant among girls in the 'thirties: there was not much chance of that. There were many jobs where young women had to hand in their notice on getting married, so the rules were laid down. The priorities were usually a husband, home and children. We are living in a totally changed world today.

Chapter Seven

In this era small shops opened and closed as was felt necessary, and as a consequence many were open till "all hours". Seeing that we lived so close to the shop, it was eight o'clock or nine o'clock some nights when Dad locked up and even as late as ten o'clock on certain occasions.

I would like to have kept on with my job at Woolworths but in 1936 a change was imminent yet again in my way of life. It was a case of doing what was best for my parents and furthering Dad's ambition to extend the business which he had started, so I didn't really have a choice.

It came about like this. Dad had a friend who owned two shops in town and was a butcher by trade. He had bought some land from the council in West Avenue, Rudheath, and was toying with the idea of building two small lock-up shops on it. There was many a debate about it between my mother and father, for Mr. Arnold had offered Dad the first chance to occupy one of the shops if the plans came to fruition.

Mother was not eager to take up these suggestions of expanding the business. She much preferred to work behind the scenes and not be "on show in a shop" standing behind the counter. In the event Dad turned to me for help when the shops were finished and I found myself installed as it were, selling fruit and vegetables and, later, groceries.

In the first place we set to work to clean the shop out ready to serve our first customer, washing the red tile floor, cleaning the large shop window and making it look attractive by polishing apples and other fruit and piling them in pyramids: generally setting out our stall, so to speak. There was no need for cooling cabinets at this stage, only lots of shelves to contain tinned fruit and vegetables. Sacks of potatoes, with the scales at the ready, were left outside the shop front. None of us knew how things would go; it was an unknown quantity and a big step to take for a very small business. Dad took a positive view as usual. There were only two shops in the long avenue at this time and one was part post-office. From the very late 'twenties onwards, many houses had been built around this area which extended the avenues eventually into a large estate, and it was quite a while before more shops were built. The one adjoining ours was let to a lady who sold baby clothes, knitting wools and haberdashery. She lived locally as I did.

Gradually we built up a good little business. I knew many of our customers, having lived in the area since I was a small child. Dad, of course, had kept on with his round after explaining the whys and wherefores of buying and selling. Incidentally, he had said when I first set out, that if I felt like helping myself to an apple (he knew I was fond of them) to just only one because even the loss of one would take profit from the others.

The lady who occupied the shop next door, when she brewed up in the middle of the afternoon, would bring a cup of tea to the back door for me, spying her chance when she thought it was quiet. Sometimes I didn't get the chance to drink it until it had gone cold: you could be experiencing a lull for a short while when suddenly everyone seemed to decide to come shopping at the same time. I preferred to be busy though, for the time passed much more quickly.

When the shops were first built our family lived down the other end of the avenue. Then Dad had a brain-wave. He thought how much handier it would be if we lived nearer the shop. They didn't particularly want to uproot us, but Mum and Dad agreed it would be better in the long run. Acting upon this idea, a letter was sent to the Council explaining everything and asking permission to move closer to the shop if and when a house became available. Surprisingly, we hadn't long to wait before we moved into a house next door but one to the shop. I was on the door-step after I had closed at one o'clock ready for my lunch. Now and again a customer might come in on the last lap, but they were pretty good on the whole, having got used to me closing the shop at one.

The next door neighbours were an old couple. The husband had a large beard which covered most of his face, most striking in appearance. People soon had a nickname for him: they called him "Lord Melchett". Actually, I always thought that he favoured Ludwig Mond, one of the founders of Brunner Mond and Co (which became ICI) from the old photos I had seen of him in the town. As time went by our neighbour placed statues in his small back garden and it was soon filled with these ornaments.

My sister Edith was sent to his house with a message on one occasion. He came to the front door and said, on seeing the little girl: "I'm just cutting my wife's toe-nails." This statement and his imposing figure startled Edith and she ran off. Nothing would induce her to go back again. There seemed to be more eccentric characters about, once upon a time.

In this era small shops opened and closed as was felt necessary, and as a consequence many were open till "all hours". Seeing that we lived so close to the shop, it was eight o'clock or nine o'clock some nights when Dad locked up and even as late as ten o'clock on certain occasions. Most small shops lingered on as long as customers turned up to be served. Of course if it wasn't worth using the electricity, the shop would be closed. We got used to people's requirements, but for small businesses it could be a very long day.

Dad would take over from me after tea when I wanted to go out with Jim, but there would usually be one night when I took over again to give him a break. I would be busy putting goods on the shelves and be ready to serve the customers who came straggling in while Jim read his newspaper and brewed up for us in the little kitchen at the back of the shop. There was a small black-leaded grate which was used when the weather was cold. We had a coal bunker in the yard at the back and a cheerful little fire in the grate with a kettle singing on the hob. During the day and evening we could always enjoy a "cuppa".

A rep called regularly from a Manchester firm which Dad dealt with. He would call in the evening when there was not much doing, and we could give him an order in a more leisurely way than during the day when we were much busier. The gentleman was always dressed in a black overcoat and a black homburg hat. He was also very large in height and breadth. The firm he represented had a name something like "Raven

Mill and Co" if I remember rightly and his black-clad appearance reminded me of a raven. Yet unlike his personal appearance, which looked rather forbidding, he was a very nice man. Dad and I would give him our order and he would tell us if there were any bargains to be had. Later he would linger on chatting with Dad and enjoy a cup of tea. I would be gone home by then with other things to do.

Mum and I found the situation so comical when, each time a box of dried peas was ordered, containing a gross of packets, a man's necktie was included free with the order. These were made of cotton and were of rather subdued colours. As time went by Mother was giving them away and this went on for ages: they weren't particularly attractive and there were still a few that turned up in a drawer a few years later. Another company gave us each a glass plate marking the Coronation of George VI in 1937. I still have mine.

Dad dealt with the firm of Morris and Jones for many years. Their representative was a Mr. Jones, too – Tudor Jones, to be exact. Of course, it was a Welsh firm. There were other reps as time went by, and they were always willing to take a small business's order without hassle, ready to oblige and put matters right if there was anything amiss.

Customers often had their groceries "on tick" (a well-known phrase) from one week to the next. Most of them were very honest and paid what they owed, and it was a pleasure to deal with them. On the other hand, one or two people regularly complained of being hard-up (and who was well-off in the 'thirties?) and after promising faithfully to pay their debts would have a sad excuse ready the following week. Soft-hearted Dad would let them have another order after listening to their tales of woe. This got to be a regular occurrence until a large sum of money was owed. In the end it was left to my mother to summon up her courage to knock on the culprit's door and ask for the money. This was quite embarrassing for her but she stuck to her guns, especially when she found out that the person in question had ordered goods including 'best butter' and other expensive items. The injustice of it acted as a spur to Mother, who would say: "I can't afford 'best butter,' for us and there's a lot of other things I'd like, but our bills have to be paid" so in the end a stop was put to this sort of thing.

The land at the back of the shop adjoined Walkers' field – that's what we called it as children. Mr. Walker's farm was situated along Shipbrook Road. When we first went to live in the Avenues, there was a running stream which separated this particular meadow from the other fields around. Probably it was no more than a wide ditch, but the water was clear and unpolluted and as a consequence water cress flourished here and there and Lady's Smocks lined its edges. We spent many a happy hour playing around and proving to one another that we could leap cross it where it widened out. I remember one afternoon especially, when I was aged about eleven, climbing a tree which overhung the ditch. I was a tomboy and counted climbing trees as one of my pastimes. There were other children in the field, including my young sister who insisted on following me no matter how hard I tried to put her off. I knew that if she tried to jump over the water she would at least get her feet wet through (she was only six at the time) and we would both be in trouble when we got home.

Instead of this happening, a girl roughly the same age as myself fell into the wide ditch. Although it was not deep it was deep enough to soak her clothing from the waist down. On seeing this happen I came down from the tree pretty quickly and helped her out. She was quite distressed because for one thing she was wearing navy blue woollen knickers which being soaking wet were heavy with ditch-water and impeded her progress. She slid them off and was quite upset as I took her home. She handed them over to me and I held them with my finger and thumb as they dripped all the way to her house at the top of the Avenue. Her mother was so grateful that I had helped her daughter to come safely home that she gave me a sixpenny piece. I felt a bit guilty at receiving this coin, had the truth be known, for the girl had been watching my antics and trying to copy them. She was an only child and I had never seen her playing this far from her own garden before. When more houses were being built in the latter part of the 1920s, this stream – or ditch – was filled in.

Chapter Eight

In Witton Street, Northwich, there was a small furniture shop owned by a Mr. Wright. He and his brother made some of their own furniture as well as selling ready-made. It was here that Jim and I went to buy the furniture for our home, bit by bit, until we had most of what we required.

*N*ow that Jim had a job at last, our spirits were uplifted. We could plan ahead for our future and life took on a rosier aspect.

Although wages were low, the cost of living was too. Things were balanced because food, clothing, furniture and so on were extremely cheap to buy by today's standards. The price of most goods stayed stable for long periods of time but I remember when the price of a loaf of bread rose from 4d to 4½d there was much mumbling and grumbling. It's now hardly credible to think that one could buy a bedroom suite for say £40 or less, which was well-made and would last for years. So it was with all that was needed to furnish one's home.

When a friend of mine got married and was setting up house, she and her husband travelled to Liverpool to look round the shops for furniture. She told me that there were bedroom suites for as low as £12. My friend decided that she wanted one that cost £19 and her husband replied: "I'm not a millionaire."

In Witton Street, Northwich, there was a small furniture shop owned by a Mr. Wright. He and his brother made some of their own furniture as well as selling ready-made. It was here that Jim and I went to buy the furniture for our home, bit by bit, until we had most of what we required. I have kept the large wardrobe from our original bedroom suite, which is in very good condition after all these years. But this came later. For the present we were enjoying being able to go to Manchester now and again too have a look round the shops and visit the cinema occasionally.

When autumn approached, Blackpool Illuminations were in full swing and we booked to go on one of the coach trips. When we arrived there the crowds were enormous as we walked along the Promenade to view the lights. It was more like being hustled and bustled along, especially when we entered the shops later. Once inside, it was difficult to get out again on to the pavement.

At this time, one of the most popular songs that you seemed to hear everywhere you went was "Carolina Moon". It was a catchy and romantic tune and enamel brooches in the form of a crescent moon were being sold everywhere. Jim bought me one and I wore it on my beret, as was the fashion. Then we found a small studio where we had our photographs taken. For some reason we both looked serious, which was unusual for Jim at any rate. It was a happy-go-lucky outing as I remember it, but we were both tired out. We didn't arrive home until one o'clock in the morning. We never visited Blackpool again until years later when we took our small daughter Vivien to see the lights. This time was a wash-out, literally. It teemed with rain the whole time we were there.

Back to the business – which was thriving. Dad gave me the job of going for eggs every Thursday afternoon, at two o'clock sharp, while Mum took over from me in the shop. She never minded because we were never long away. Charlie Barber would come along in his taxi to pick me up with my large wooden crates in which the trays of eggs were stacked. We went to a farm near Byley to collect them.

Charlie was a mechanic who had started up a small business with his wife Dorothy. The business was only in its infancy at this time but I remember that they both worked extremely hard. I think that Mrs. Barber did the book-keeping and paperwork while her husband repaired cars and other vehicles. After years of hard work they bought a large garage and house along Middlewich Road in Rudheath, and the business flourished. They are both dead now of course but they would be very proud of the way the firm which they founded has gone from strength to strength, having been handed down to their family.

On numerous occasions when I had been visiting Jim's family, he and I would walk back to Rudheath via 'Roker'. It was always abbreviated like that by local people, but now it's known as 'Roker Park' and has a leisure area and a lovely flower garden. When I was in my teens, it consisted of meadows which surrounded the River Dane and came as far as the railway arches at Leftwich. On our way home we would call at a small shop in London Road where I would be treated to my favourite sweets, buttered brazil nuts (Barker and Dobson's, I think). They were large and gorgeous: no chocolates stood so high in my estimation as these. As years went by they became smaller and less delicious, and now they seem to have disappeared altogether. We would then set off, arm in arm, as happy as two people could be.

Twelve months had passed since Jim had once more become an earner of a weekly wage, and now we wanted to get engaged. His parents had been most lenient in helping him to get on his feet, and we always appreciated this. Now he was able to buy me a ring. It was 18 carat gold and only cost about £5, but the jeweller in town assured us that the tiny diamonds were the real thing. I bought Jim a gold signet ring and had 'J' and 'L' engraved on it.

At this time, during the nice weather, Jim would play bowls at the Bowling Green Inn, taking part in matches and competitions, eventually winning the Kennedy Silver Cup and a hallmarked solid gold and silver medal which today is very valuable. This presentation coincided with the beginning of our marriage and the cup took pride of place on our sideboard in 1937.

Jim had always been very fond of fishing and helped his Dad in the 'weighing in' at matches along the River Weaver when he was a young lad. Now and again we would walk as far as Hunt's Lock on a fishing expedition. My Dad never enjoyed it – he thought it most boring – whereas Jim liked the peacefulness of the situation.

The winters were a different thing, and could be drastic for people like Jim who was afflicted with bronchitis. He would have one bad bout of it most winters when the weather turned nasty with fog creeping around which often turned into smog. There would be an acrid taste in your mouth from the mixture of fog and the smoke from coal fires. It was hard not to breathe it in. I remember one time when a young lad brought a message from Jim to tell me he was in bed with the 'flu, unable to come to see me, and asking if I would come to him. Neither of us could know that the weather would turn into a real 'pea-souper', as this horrible smog was known. I went in the early evening when, although it was foggy, it wasn't too bad – just patchy in places. But when I returned it became thicker as I groped my way to the bus terminus and stepped on to the last bus to run that night. In those days it was normal for people to pass one another in the street and hardly recognise each other, so thick could the fog become. It gave one an eerie feeling on these occasions, when all sound became muted by the thick fog and people seemed to move like wraiths from another world. Of course, it was then a case of stopping indoors if possible, until the fog lifted.

About this time my sister had acquired another job. She went to be housemaid to a couple who lived in a semi-detached house in School Lane, Hartford, where she lived in. Actually she was expected to do all and sundry, for a wage which would be classed as 'peanuts' in modern terms. She was not much more than fifteen years of age, but worked very hard. The lady of the house was meticulous in every way; she appeared to be the essence of perfection. In her lunch break Edie would walk down to the old stone bridge over the River Weaver, come back to Sandstone Lodge which stood just inside the path to Vale Royal Abbey, walk past the lodge for about a quarter of a mile and then return, because she told us how lonely and rather spooky it was with trees and high shrubs bordering the path. After working, or should I say 'slaving', there for six months, the crunch came when... *(Lenna never finished this sentence when she was revising her manuscript).*

My birthday falls on November 26 and I found it quite a coincidence when we realised that Jim's birthday was the day before mine, and his brother's the day after.

As I was nearing my 21st birthday my mother organised a small party for both our families. I bought a dress from my next door neighbour at the shop. I remember that it was a lovely shade of primrose yellow with white trimmings and I felt really smart in it. Dad only paid me a small wage at the time for serving in the shop, but he and my mother were very good to me in lots of ways and I was never refused anything that I really wanted.

My present from Jim was a Lloyd Loom linen basket. Embroidered on the lid it had a garden scene with a lady in a crinoline dress standing amid flowers, covered with thick glass. These old-fashioned scenes were very popular and could often be seen painted on mirrors and so on. The linen basket is still in use, as good as ever, which speaks well of the firm who made it.

Sifting through old photographs recently I found one of me, sitting in my sister-in-law's garden holding what at first glance appears to be a bunch of flowers, but on closer inspection turns out to be a cream-coloured Pekingese dog with its fur fluffed up and waving a feathery tail. I could not believe that I would ever be capable of holding what I privately thought of as 'that little monster'. When I first used to visit the house, this little dog, which seemed to look disdainfully upon me, would sit by my side on the sofa all the while I was there. I was petrified because it watched me constantly with its bulging eyes not unlike marbles. Woe betide me if I moved. The family was besotted with this dog, which had a pedigree as long as your arm, and had called it 'Cutie'. The time would come when I just had to get towards the door if I wanted to go home, whereupon it would leap from the sofa dashing to catch me before I left, yapping and snapping at my heels. No amount of crying 'Cutie come here.' would induce it to stop until it was picked up bodily. A long while passed before it accepted me, but eventually it did.

I must state here that Edie and I were not used to animals, especially dogs, although my mother did have one attempt at keeping a cat when we were young children. It was black with white 'socks' and we named it 'Snooker' after a cartoon character in the Daily Sketch newspaper. We were very fond of it, but one day it wandered off and never came back. We were so upset that Mother never kept a cat again.

One Saturday afternoon Jim and I called in at Gee's shop in town to put a deposit on two New Hudson bikes complete with three speed gears. And although I can hardly describe it as a dream come true, it fulfilled a longing I had always had for a bike of my own. To me it was synonymous with independence and we came away from the shop envisaging many miles of travel. When it came to the crunch, we hadn't the time to journey long distances, but we certainly used the machines extensively for jaunts which gave us much pleasure, and we had them for many years.

We knew Mr. and Mrs. Gee before they were married. They had been bike enthusiasts for years, but I think an accident had curtailed their activities in that direction. Later they set up a small business in Witton Street, Northwich. Mr. Gee knew all there was to know about cycling and the business flourished. I believe his son-in-law owns a much larger shop, now.

Chapter Nine

I had kept the excitement I felt about our wedding at low key up to now, trying to get on with my work, but in the end I felt as most young girls do, nervous and yet thrilled at the prospect of a new way of life stretching before me.

CHAPTER NINE

*I*n 1936 we saw the abdication of Edward VIII, although there had been no coronation, and I remember the ill-feeling at the time that was engendered when he let it be known that he wanted Mrs. Simpson to share the throne with him. Now in 1937 his younger brother the Duke of York was forced to take on the responsibility of being King in his place. He was crowned in May along with Queen Elizabeth, now the Queen Mother, in Westminster Abbey, to much acclaim. This was an auspicious year for Jim and me because we were planning to get married.

We sought out Mr. Wright, our local councillor. I looked upon him as a benefactor for after consultation with him and explaining our hopes for the future, he lent his considerable influence towards our application for a council house in East Avenue. This was granted, and we paid the rent on it for almost three months, bit by bit furnishing it with most of the things we required, before we got married. The rent, by the way, cost us the princely sum of 5/6d per week. We remained there for 21 years, and our very good neighbours consecutively were from two branches of the same Stanley family.

We juggled about the wedding date until it was suitable for all concerned and finally decided on June 21, 1937. The marriage was to be on a Monday which was a quiet day when Dad could close the shop without too much hassle. My mother and I were occupied with thoughts of the wedding – a 'white' one that we could look back on with pride and pleasure. Mum and Dad wanted it to be as good as possible for me, not a large affair, but special. There was not a big selection of bridal clothes in Northwich, so eventually Mother acquired a clothing catalogue from the Yorkshire firm of J G Graves. They were said to be noted for their quality and reliability, and so it turned out to be.

Naturally I spent as much time as I could leafing through the pages until I decided what I wanted. Very fashionable in 1937 were white satin ankle-length close-fitting dresses which flared

63

out slightly at the hem. This style suited me very well and this was the design I chose. It had a slight cowl neckline and long tight-fitting sleeves. The belt that went with it was much too long and had to be taken in. The wedding veil just touched the ground and was held by a wreath of orange blossom round my head. I had white silk stockings (no such material as nylon in those days) and white satin high-heeled shoes. Altogether the effect was very attractive without being fussy.

My mother paid cash on delivery when my outfit arrived and I was delighted with it. She dealt with J G Graves for several years afterwards; I think they were in business until few years ago. The rest of my trousseau was now complete and I had everything I needed. There had been times when both Jim and I had been despondent, wondering if ever the situation would alter for the better, but we had weathered the storm and now looked forward with optimism to our future together.

Plans went ahead for our wedding. We visited the vicars of Davenham and Witton to arrange for the banns to be read in each church, because Jim lived in the parish of Davenham and I in Witton. When I was a child it had been the other way round, and we who now lived in Rudheath had belonged to Davenham parish.

There was an event being held in St John's Room (the infants' school stood next door at that time) on June 21 so Dad was unable to book it for us as had been intended. In the end he arranged for us to hold our celebration in the large upstairs room at the old Farmer's Arms. Various of our shop customers brought me presents and wished me much happiness; most of them I had known for many years. There is a large influx of strangers to Rudheath now, but during the times of which I am writing there was not much moving around. Families would stay in the same houses for ages.

As June 21 approached we went to Dean's the jewellers in Witton Street to buy the wedding ring. We climbed up the spiral staircase to the room where we were shown all types of rings. Thin gold bands were the new fashion and I chose one that was faceted with tiny platinum orange blossoms engraved on it. Many years later I removed it for the first time. It had become tight on my finger and Jim replaced it with a thick gold band. Of course I treasure my original wedding ring. Last minute arrangements were now in place, visits from relatives dealt with and 'the Day' was almost upon us.

I had kept the excitement I felt at low key up to now, trying to get on with my work, but in the end I felt as most young girls do, nervous and yet thrilled at the prospect of a new way of life stretching before me. I had eagerly opened up the layers of tissue paper that enfolded my wedding dress and veil, when they had been delivered, and now they were hanging safely in the wardrobe ready for 'the Day'. I took yet another look at them and had mixed emotions. Firstly the fact that after the morrow I would be a married woman with the responsibility that this entailed, and also knowing that Jim and I would be together for ever. All these thoughts went through my mind as I drifted off into sleep on the eve of my wedding day.

June 21, 1937 dawned fine but rather hazy. Dad went to open the shop at nine o'clock while Mother and I occupied ourselves with various chores. Relatives called to wish me happiness and soon it was time to get dressed in all my finery and to choose 'something old, something new, something borrowed, something blue'. I think that a lace hanky was the 'borrowed' bit and the 'something blue' was a fancy garter. Girls wore them to keep their stockings up when going somewhere special and they were very fashionable. After dinner Dad went for a drink and kept us all on tenterhooks by staying out longer than he intended. He came dashing back home looking very happy.

In the end we were ready with a little time to spare. I had been too occupied to even look out through the window so as I stepped out holding onto Dad's arm, I had a nice shock, for outside our gate were quite a number of people whom I had known since childhood, and customers, gathered to wish me luck. As usual I felt rather embarrassed at being taken by surprise, but also pleased that they wanted to show me their goodwill. Dad helped me into the waiting car as I held my bouquet of lovely pale yellow roses in one hand and the long delicate veil over my arm. We settled back and then with good wishes lingering in our ears we set off for Witton Church.

We followed wedding tradition by walking up to the church porch not through the lych gate but via a side gate. The sun was shining, a gentle breeze lifted my veil, and June 21, the longest day in the calendar, was a beautiful day. We walked down the aisle and I took my place beside Jim. He turned to look at me, gently squeezed my hand to give me reassurance, and soon the marriage service began. There were no wedding bells ringing, no professional photographer to take our photos, but everyone was present who meant anything to us and the whole ceremony, which was conducted by the Vicar of Lostock, the Rev Sidney Evans (the resident vicar being away), was filled with a feeling of love and deep commitment between Jim and me which never left us – in spite of the fact that there would be times when life would not be at all easy.

As we came out of the church porch, my cousin Jean presented me with a silver and satin horseshoe for good luck.

Afterwards, as we all made our way to celebrate the occasion, everyone was looking forward to enjoying a good 'feast' – and that is what it proved to be. But first of all we gathered on the bowling green at the Farmer's Arms so that an aunt could take snaps of us with a Kodak box camera. Among those present was my grandfather, who was 85 years old on that day. I had two bridesmaids, my twelve-year-old sister and a cousin. They looked so pretty in their turquoise dresses, wearing headbands of silvery leaves and carrying Victorian posies. I also had a maid of honour, Jim's sister, who wore a dress of pale pink voile that fell in soft folds around her – very stylish – and carried a large bouquet. All these dresses had small sprigs of flowers in the design of the material, which was very appropriate for the time of year. Various souvenir photographs were taken of Jim and me, the best man, maid of honour, bridesmaids and members of our families – all beaming into the camera. As one film was removed, another was put in its place in the camera.

It was a small but picturesque white wedding and we were proud because not many people like us were able to have them during the 'thirties. Through thick and thin we had waited years for such a perfect day and we looked forward to seeing the photographs. In the end there were none because the person who was responsible for this part of the proceedings overexposed them, 'let in the light' or did something else drastically wrong. This always rankled with us as years went by when we saw other people's photos. Ours had been such a lovely wedding and there is no pictorial record of it at all...

Of course at the time we were unaware that anything was wrong and after all the posing, we trooped upstairs to the big room at the Arms, to find a welcome feast laid out for us. It looked very inviting with our wedding cake as the centre of attention. Just before we took our places at the table, there was a slight commotion at the window and someone said, "Somebody outside wants to speak to you, Lenna – and Jim as well." The sash window was pulled up and as I leant forward an object was handed up to us on a long pole. It was a chamber pot arrayed with pink ribbons and all around the outside was written in black paint a poem about a greengrocer's daughter. It was composed by a neighbour all in good fun, and everyone seemed to think it hilarious and a wonderful idea. I just wished the earth would swallow me up. I left others to read the lines but thankfully they turned out not to be rude or offensive and we then turned our attention to the table.

My grandmother, whom I had loved dearly, had died in 1931 at the age of 71 and of course I wished that she had been able to be with me on my wedding day. Then I remembered that on her golden wedding day she had given me a gold ring decoration from her own wedding cake which had a small white dove attached to it. I had kept it ever since and decided that it should be incorporated into the rest of the decoration on our cake.

After we had eaten, drunk the toasts and received the greetings telegrams (from my brother-in-law who was away on holiday, a workmate of Jim's and my cousins) we all chatted and then dispersed later in the afternoon, promising to return in the evening for another get-together. After I went home to change out of my finery and into something more casual, I found that there was a small rip in my wedding veil. I then recalled that my sister-in-law – who was a tiny person – had stepped on to the end of my veil as it touched the ground. I had felt a slight tug but did not realise at the time that the very high heels that she was wearing had cut through the gauzy material. I wrapped it up carefully with its waxy wreath of orange blossom, with the intention of having it repaired at a later date. Jim and I then walked to Witton Church to lay my lovely bouquet on Granny's grave.

More people came in the evening to our 'do' than were expected but they all seemed to enjoy it. We had a neighbour, Jim Dakin, who played the piano-accordion very professionally, and he provided the music while we danced. I say 'danced' with care – speaking for ourselves neither Jim nor I were very good exponents of waltzing or dancing in general. In fact we had never had much chance to participate in such pastimes because we couldn't afford to go to the local dances. Nevertheless most guests stayed on until it was quite late; as for us we moved towards my old home with a few relatives and both lots of parents. There was drink provided for those who wanted it but my mother ended up brewing pots of tea for most of us. By now it was almost midnight and we left for our own home. The night was quite beautiful and not totally dark. In distance it was only a stone's throw from my parents' house but to us it was a world apart. You know the familiar phrase, 'an Englishman's home is his castle', and so it was for us.

I have been using a china cup and saucer that I bought recently. It has a delicate design of violets painted on it and as I write these words it has brought back with great clarity the first day of our married life together. I set the breakfast table with just such a set of china. As my mind reaches back in time not only can I see us sitting there together, but I also get the feeling of strangeness and happiness that encompassed me as I began a new chapter in my life.

Jim had a week's holiday. We hadn't the money to go 'gallivanting off' so we enjoyed pottering about, he in the garden putting in order the lovely crimson rambling roses which the previous tenant had left us, that had grown rather wild, and me playing at 'house', as I fondly recall, for everything was new to me then. During the course of the week the silver cup that Jim had won was presented to him and I arranged it in pride of place on the sideboard.

Once a week the insurance man would call. He was a second cousin of Jim's and although the insurance we took out was only small it was a good investment due to his sound advice. He knew that our means were limited. He duly admired the silver sup which was there on the sideboard when he first called on us, and he enjoyed a cup of tea regularly thereafter as he chatted to Jim. We were lucky that my parents had a grocery business. They were very kind to us in lots of ways when, as time passed, the tannery business began to decline – a sign of things to come.

Chapter Ten

When I look back I think that we were very
fortunate to experience such happiness. For
ordinary folk like us, there was not a sign of war on
the horizon — we would have been horrified at the
suggestion — yet twelve months later all had
changed and things would never be the same again.

A year later our first daughter was born – in June 1938. My in-laws were positive that our baby would be a boy, seeming to know the signs (whatever they were), and I naively believed them. When 'she' was born I had no girls' names ready and so what should she be but 'June'? My pregnancy had been completely trouble-free apart from the usual morning sickness but at the very last things got difficult. The midwife that I knew well and liked had been called out to attend the birth of a baby boy shortly before I needed her, and we were forced to call out a nurse from Lostock in the middle of the night. She said she had gone to bed with a cold – but we soon found out that it had been a with a bottle of whisky. Consequently she was too befuddled to realise when events took a dangerous turn. Through the small hours of the night I suffered a great deal of unnecessary pain and when my own nurse was free she took no time in sending for our doctor who lived in Middlewich Road. Dr Bent arrived at about 6.30 on Whit Monday morning. He spoke reassuringly to me and administered a dose of ether through a mask over my face. I was asleep in the twinkling of an eye. All I remember next is Dr Bent's voice saying, "She's coming to, she's smiling", which was no wonder since all my agony had disappeared. I was presented with a red-faced baby girl, who had been delivered by forceps, yelling loudly and whose features strongly resembled Jim's side of the family. We thanked God for our doctor, for without his help I could not have brought our baby into the world – indeed, one or both of us might have died. I went to sleep almost immediately, naturally this time, and when I awoke I saw my husband tenderly holding her. All had returned to peace and quiet.

There was no getting out of bed shortly after having a baby and resuming one's duties – not in the 'thirties. We were advised to stay in bed at least a week, the midwife having fastened a long piece of cotton material, or ideally a bolster case, around one's stomach a couple of days after the birth. I presume this was to strengthen you and get you into shape.

Because it was June, Rudheath fête was in full swing and I knelt up in bed (we weren't supposed to put a foot to the floor) to try to watch the procession as it passed by our house. It was a big affair at that time, with dancing troupes from various towns taking part, competing for the silver shield and money prizes. I felt that I wanted to be outside and not in bed but I did as the nurse instructed me and after a week I was up and about again, feeling fine. How life has altered. Nowadays young women are expected to go into hospital to have their babies and are usually up again the next day.

Our life now settled into a happy and calm routine. I looked after the baby and our home while Jim worked hard to earn a living for us. When some of the men were laid off for want of orders coming in to Dutton's Tannery, he was given a job of gardening up at the boss's house, so he was never out of work. Business picked up again after several weeks, but I think it was a warning that things were not boding too well for the future. There had always been a big demand in the past for leather goods but change was on the way.

Sometimes we went for walks down Shipbrook Road. It was pleasant sitting on the railings at the bottom of the hill where the 'Gad' brook joins the River Dane, the baby fast asleep as usual and both of us munching a bar of chocolate, then afterwards pushing the pram up the steep hill on our way home. When I look back I think that we were very fortunate to experience such happiness. For ordinary folk like us, there was not a sign of war on the horizon – we would have been horrified at the suggestion – yet twelve months later all had changed and things would never be the same again.

In the meanwhile we had a job, a small happy home of our own, and a family. Now and again Jim would be asked to work overtime on Saturday afternoons, when more orders came in, but at other times we would go to town. When Witton Street became crowded with shoppers it was sometimes a bit difficult to manoeuvre a way through, babies' prams being much larger than they are today. Jim would say: "We could do with a bell on this pram handle", then "Watch me mow my way through.". We thought this was very funny because he was the least aggressive of men.

In that first summer, Jim would go straight to his parents' home from work and I would meet him there. Once a week we would have our tea with them and enjoy their company until late in the evening. Then we would return home, he pushing his bike and me pushing the pram. They were lovely quiet times as we walked up through Roker Park back to Rudheath. It came back to us via someone's gossip that we were being criticised for "keeping that child out late". Somebody had seen us. If only they could have seen June. She would be fast asleep and oblivious to everything as I prepared to put her in her cot, and would remain so throughout the night. From the very first, she knew what was good for her, and progressed accordingly.

My friend Mary from our schooldays and Clarence her husband moved into a house opposite us, and she had a baby daughter the same age as ours. (In many ways our lives ran parallel through the years. Our girls went on to Grammar School at the age of 11, our husbands went into business eventually, and our grandsons both work for Rolls-Royce at Crewe in the same department).

On Sundays we sometimes went for drives on the Cheshire lanes with my parents. I remember one afternoon in early summer when we took a picnic in the woods at Oulton Park. The Hall which had stood there had been burned down some time before. It was a beautiful day as we relaxed in the fresh air. Suddenly we heard a cuckoo calling somewhere quite close to us, but unseen, then again in the distance, and so it went on for most of the afternoon. There is now a motor racing circuit in the grounds and I doubt if it would be so peaceful nowadays when the loud noise of revving engines takes place.

Our first Christmas with the baby, who was now six months old, was approaching. She was the only grandchild and would be for the next nine years. My mother was delighted and quite set up with her title of 'Granny' even though she was only in her early forties, and my sister, who was 17, was now 'Aunt Edie'.

Christmas with all the trappings of brightness, colour and normality soon passed and before we knew it we were into the year 1939, a year which would prove ominous and have devastating consequences for all of us.

As I write I am searching my memory for times past, and I recollect the first Easter for our little girl, who was now...

Part Two
by June Hall

*L*enna did not complete that sentence. Did she leave her writing to answer the telephone or to make a cup of tea, in her cup with the violets, while she continued to search her memory? Or did she feel too tired just then? We shall never know.

For by then, the autumn of 1999, she was on her own. Her writing and painting were her consolation. The success of her first book never failed to amaze her. It was published a few weeks after Dad died and the contact it brought her kept her going through the saddest time of her life. Encouraged by the demand for *Memories of a Cheshire Childhood* she continued her story, with the intention of finishing with the outbreak of World War II. After the War and the years of separation it brought, she felt that life had changed for ever.

So, it is left to me to complete her account. I don't know what she intended to say about me, in her last sentence – their "little girl". All I know of this time comes from the reminiscences of Mum and Granny as they talked fondly of "the baby", in these calm days before the storm of war. And as I became aware of the world around me, I can recall something of the atmosphere of life lived modestly, decently and in a caring, hardworking family. This is not my story, however, and all I want to do is complete Lenna's own.

We can return to her, a young married woman, her dream of a home and family of her own come true. The house was small, with a living room, a kitchen (referred to as the scullery), a larder with a stone slab for keeping food cool, and a bathroom. Upstairs were two bedrooms. The lavatory was outside at this time. The red tiled floors of the ground floor were treated weekly with Cardinal, a rich, red polish, and the furniture gleamed with Mansion Polish. In the living room, a coal-fired range with an oven and boiler, provided heat and cooking facilities.

The kitchen had a small electric hob and grill. There was also a boiler for laundry, with its own coal fire and chimney. Lenna had attended "housewifery" classes as a young girl and was pleased to cook and clean, wash and iron, with considerable skill. Her volume of *Mrs. Beeton* contained all she needed, to run her home.

Washdays were quite challenging. Out came the galvanised dolly tubs, the dolly stick, buckets, mangle with heavy wooden rollers and great iron cog-wheels, the scrubbing brushes, Fairy soap, Oxydol powder and Dolly Blue. Bed linen and other "whites" were soaked, boiled, scrubbed, rinsed and wrung, as steam filled the house and the smell of laundry was inescapable. Then came the drying. On fine days, the line full of billowing washing was a joy – arms full of sweet-smelling clothes could be gathered and folded ready for ironing – but on wet days it hung around the house for ages. In the freezing weather of winter, sheets as stiff as boards made hands red and chapped. Whatever the time of year, heaps of clean clothes were ready to be ironed – another great performance.

Flat irons were heated on the hob, picked up with padded holders and rubbed across a cake of soap to make them glide smoothly. The final process was airing, done on the clothes "maiden". Damp clothes and bedding were an ever-present worry in homes without any form of heating other than one coal fire. Pneumonia, tuberculosis and bronchitis were especially dangerous in these days before the introduction of antibiotics. Jim's tendency to chest colds made Mum extremely careful to air laundry.

The two bedrooms were cold places, but the larger one had its own little cast-iron fireplace. This was only lit in times of illness. Then, a shovel full of lighted coals from the downstairs fireplace was brought up to provide an instant source of warmth.

My parents' bedroom as I remember it, was as they had furnished it for their marriage. With windows to east and west, it was a light and airy room. The bed, wardrobe, dressing table and tallboy were, as Mum has written, of walnut, a pale golden wood, in Art Deco style. The dressing table had triple mirrors, hinged, to give side and even back views. An amber-coloured glass dressing-table set (tray, candlesticks and pots with lids) was arranged on hand-crocheted mats. The other ornament in the room stood on the tallboy. It was a figurine of a dark-haired lady in a long red dress, dancing. This is the room where I was born.

Downstairs in the living room, were the dining table and leather-seated chairs of dark oak. Two fireside chairs, which could be adjusted to recline, took their place either side of the hearth. A little desk, referred to as the bureau, also of dark oak, held books on its shelves beneath the desk compartment. Inside were the few items of household business; a black and gilt tin cashbox, the rent book, insurance books, birth and marriage certificates and our identity cards.

There was a small, square table with barley-sugar legs, which was used to hold a vase of flowers, or the little artificial Christmas tree. Apparently the tree was bought for my first Christmas, when I was six months old, and was decorated with glass baubles and tiny red wax candles in clip-on holders. When I was held up to see the tree, I managed to take hold of a branch and pulled the whole thing over, shattering some of the baubles.

There were several stools in the house. One was also a box of padded leather, used to hold our slippers. Another was a barley-sugar legged, square stool, with a seat of woven sea grass. The third was a sturdy, traditional wooden stool, with a hole in the top, for picking it up. Dad had made this, and it has outlasted most of the other furniture.

The garden was Dad's delight. A neat lawn at the front was surrounded by a border in which he planted annuals and bulbs. Beside the path, marguerites and montbretia flourished. Privet hedges formed the boundary and a lime tree stood where our garden adjoined our neighbour's, near the road. Each year, the lime trees which formed the "Avenues" were severely pollarded. For a while, in winter, they looked stumpy and inelegant, but when spring came, they soon grew into their leafy beauty.

Behind the house Dad grew old fashioned cottage flowers. I have never seen more beautiful, tall delphiniums of so many different shades of blue, some with creamy centres and iridescent azure petals, others of deep midnight blue with black centres. Near them grew red tea roses. A flowering currant bush and a pale lilac produced masses of scented blooms and scabious and pinks attracted butterflies. Red rambling roses, pyrethrum, geum, multi-coloured russell lupins, michaelmas daisies and purple "twelve apostles" formed a perennial background to annual delights – snapdragons, sweet peas, nemesia... There were blackcurrants (Dad's favourite fruit for jam) and rhubarb, and sometimes peas, beans, beetroot, cabbage, lettuce, radishes and outdoor tomatoes. In the shed, his tools were arranged methodically and the bicycles were stored.

This, then, was the home which Lenna and Jim established and where they lived on Jim's modest wages, until the devastating events of the War took over. Inevitably, the day came when Dad received his call-up papers. Of course I was too young to know much about these events, but Dad had to leave us and Mum, like most able-bodied women, had to fill the jobs the men had left. While Dad became part of the bomb disposal service of the Royal Engineers, Mum worked at ICI Wallerscote, in the stores of the joiners' shop. Meanwhile, I stayed with Granny and Granddad, while they ran the shop. Edie was still at home with them, a stylish young woman who curled her hair with iron tongs, heated in the fire, and who danced the "jitterbug".

During my early childhood, Dad was in the Army. My memories of him then, are reinforced by the photographs, taken on the "box Brownie", when he was home on leave. Despite the ever-present threat of invasion, and the knowledge that leave was so short, these were happy days when we went for cycle rides. I travelled on a seat fixed to Dad's crossbar and we rode round the quiet lanes of Plumley, Lach Dennis, Goostrey, Byley and Whatcroft. Sometimes we would stop at the Duke of Portland, at Lach Dennis, for a drink, sitting in the garden of the pub.

Some of my earliest memories are of visits to see Dad while he was in Yorkshire, Lincolnshire or Nottinghamshire on his dangerous work. I think the first trip Mum and I made was to Halifax. All I recall is the train journey, and the Horlicks tablets I ate on the way. Mum was not an experienced traveller and in the dark days of the War, must have been very nervous. Another time, we stayed in the village of Ketton, near Stamford, lodging with the family of Mr. Burbage, the village butcher. My clearest recollections are of staying on a farm in Grainsby, Lincolnshire. Here, I first saw a chicken hatch, sat on a swing which hung from an apple tree, and watched in amazement the night-time bombing of Grimsby, some eight miles away.

The War had a great effect on our lives. Dad was in constant danger. He was not robust and had a quiet nature. The close friends he made were all killed as they worked on unexploded bombs. He rarely talked about his experiences, but they must have been horrific. We were lucky to have him back.

At home, we carried on with our lives, but the air-raid warning, black-out, rationing and the sombre tones of Big Ben before the News on the wireless, all contributed to a tense and anxious backdrop to our daily routine. When the air-raid siren blew, there was the panic of putting on gas-masks and hurrying to the air-raid shelter. The last and worst moments of the War were the raids by Doodlebugs, the motorised bombs aimed at Manchester and Liverpool. We could hear them droning overhead, dreading silence, which would mean they would drop.

When Peace was declared and Dad was "demobbed" we could pick up the threads of family life and settle into our home again. We even had a holiday. In 1946 we went to the isle of Man for a week. As soon as we embarked on the Mona's Queen, at Liverpool, Dad disappeared. We found him below deck, suffering from seasickness, before the ship had crossed the bar in the Mersey. The crossing was stormy – one of the worst the sailors could recall. Mum and I spent the voyage out on deck, in lashing wind, waves and rain, clinging to ropes. A fleet of ambulances met the boat, as so many people had been injured. Once there, we had a wonderful week on the beaches and visiting the sights – Rushen Abbey, Groudle Glen, the Laxey Wheel, Peel Castle and Douglas, our base. I have clear memories of eating toffee apples, riding in a horse-drawn tram and going up and down on fairground horses.

Dad returned to work at the tannery. He cycled to his job, as most workmen did then. In February 1946 Northwich suffered devastating floods. A mural painting, which decorated the foyer of the Regal Cinema for many years, showed the scene. I always felt sorry for the black cat, shown floating on a plant.

Vivien was born in August 1947, in one of the hottest summers on record. When the new baby was put in the garden in her pram – a large, coach-built baby carriage with a big hood – she had to be protected from wasps, which seemed to be everywhere. Lenna's wedding veil was brought into use and draped over the pram. So now I had a little sister and our family was complete.

I was nine years old and something of a tomboy. My interests were in making things – dolls house furniture from matchboxes, knitting and sewing clothes for my dolls, and for my sister, drawing and cutting out costume dolls of historical figures. I enjoyed helping Dad in the garden, and going further afield with the local children. We climbed trees, jumped brooks and walked along the canal towpath to Billinge Green and Whatcroft. On the way we would pass several ponds where moorhens, coots, swans and great-crested grebe nested. It was fascinating to see moorhens' nests built on stilts of twigs, and

81

grebe chicks on their mothers' backs. The water plants were lovely – bullrushes, mint, various rushes, forget-me-nots and marsh marigolds. We fished with nets for sticklebacks, collected newts and frog spawn, providing them with a home for a few weeks before returning them to the wild.

At school, in the playground, and in the evenings, out of doors, we played the games which mysteriously came into season – marbles, skipping, hand-stands, jacks, yo-yo and singing games.

My first school was St John's Infant School, on Middlewich Road (now demolished), after which I went to Victoria Road Junior School in Northwich, the Council School which Granny had attended. By the time Vivien was of school age, the new primary school at Rudheath had been built and she went there. It stood in the fields behind our house – the former cornfields with little oak trees in the hedges. Every year a cuckoo came to sit in one of them and made his persistent call.

We still enjoyed the freedom that Lenna had experienced in her young life. There was little traffic as most people walked, cycled or caught the bus. Vivien was to grow up into the changing world of post-war England.

Shortly after Vivien was born, the tannery closed down. The family made a big decision, to set Dad up with a van to take fresh fruit and vegetables round Rudheath, while Granddad continued with the shop. Dad built up a regular clientele and for many years was a familiar part of the local scene. It was hard physical work, loading and unloading the van with potatoes, vegetables, fruit and tinned food; driving round the streets and walking to doors. The hours were long, starting well before 8a.m. and sometimes not returning until nine at night. On Christmas Eve, he often worked until almost midnight. There were twice-weekly journeys to Manchester wholesale market, leaving home at 4.40a.m. and returning in time to open up the shop, and local trips to farms in Goostrey, Lach Dennis and Byley for potatoes and eggs.

When the weather was fine, all was well, but many a time Dad came home drenched to the skin, to change into dry clothes, have a hot drink of tea and set off again. It is easy to forget that waterproof clothing, spin driers, central heating, double glazing and such comforts were still in the future.

Throughout the years of our childhood, Lenna and Jim worked hard, Lenna often helping Jim on the round. There was not much time, money or energy for holidays. On Sundays, after Dad had finished his week's paperwork, we often had outings. Vale Royal was still the favourite destination. We would put on our "best" clothes and catch a bus to town, change buses at the terminus and ride into Hartford. From there we walked to Monkey Lodge, Rookery Pool and back along the Weaver to the Iron Bridge. The by-pass was not completed until many years later, but the section from Hartford to Davenham had been excavated into the sandy soil. This was known as the Rubber Dump, as old wartime tyres were burned here. Our walk home took this route, and continued to Rudheath along the "New Road" past high hawthorn hedges, home to yellowhammers.

After the War, Grandpa bought a second-hand car, a wonderful, gracious old vehicle, a Humber Super Snipe. Like most cars of the time, it was black. Coloured cars were most unusual. It had running boards and deep, comfortable upholstery. As Granddad had not driven for many years, Dad became the family chauffeur, and the North Wales coast was the usual destination. Many a Sunday, we have sat for hours in traffic jams through Chester (no ring road then).

Lenna's story continued through changing times. Home life was gradually modernised and new ideas absorbed. We lived near to Granny and Granddad and were a close family. Edith, (Granny) and Lenna were to retain a very strong emotional bond throughout their lives.

Against the workaday background of life in Rudheath, over

many decades, Lenna's inner resources provided her with a wealth of rich experience. She had been a clever girl at school (apart from her horror of "sums"). The grounding she had received in the village school beside the canal widened her mental horizons and was to be a lifelong source of inspiration. She was extremely well-read in the classics, Mrs. Gaskell being her particular favourite author.

Her love of poetry was strong. As a child, she had learned reams of verse by heart and would often recite pieces which became familiar to us over the years. Among these were "Sherwood in the twilight, is Robin Hood awake?"; "Who has seen the wind? Neither you nor I"; and "Abou Ben Adam, may his tribe increase". Lenna could find great pleasure in both deeply serious and sad poetry and in lighter verse. As she grew older, she studied the works of John Clare and had enormous sympathy for the plight of a poet of such perception of the natural world, who suffered for his sensitive nature by being consigned to a madhouse. Lenna had a natural sense of fairness and found it difficult to accept or tolerate injustice at any level. This attitude eventually led her towards Quaker ways and she joined the Society of Friends in the late 1970s. She was a member of Frandley (Seven Oaks) Meeting, and took an active role in Amnesty International, at fund-raising events.

One of the most interesting events of her life occurred in 1982. That Easter, the Queen distributed the Royal Maundy at Chester Cathedral. As this was to be an ecumenical occasion, representatives of the various religious groups were invited to receive the Maundy. Mum was chosen to represent the Quakers at the ceremony, and she found it both enjoyable and moving – a chance to participate in history and tradition.

History was a great source of interest and Lenna spent long hours reading biographies. Antonia Fraser's lives of Cromwell, Mary Queen of Scots and others, fascinated her. Whenever and wherever possible, she and Jim enjoyed visits to historic houses. The local favourite was Little Moreton Hall, moated and timber-framed, in whose empty long-gallery, with panelling and plaster work, Lenna could give rein to her imagination. Haddon Hall, Chatsworth, Beeston Castle, Tatton Park, Adlington, Lyme – all these lovely old buildings fed her spirit. So too, did the ancient parish churches of Cheshire. To her great delight, a splendid book was published in 1947 *Old Cheshire Churches* by Raymond Richards. Dad bought it for her for their 13th wedding anniversary. It was to provide them with endless pleasure over the subsequent years, on their Wednesday afternoon drives into the Cheshire countryside, on Dad's half-day from work.

Although Lenna never learnt to play a musical instrument, or joined a choir, she had a great capacity for music. This originated early in her life, by means of the "wireless". She used to tell us that she listened to musical appreciation programmes which introduced her to the works of the great composers. She could remember music she heard, along with the names of composers, and the performers and conductors she enjoyed. Also, she read the lives of her favourite composers, among them Schumann, Schubert, Mendelssohn and Tchaikovsky. Above all, she loved the works of Rachmaninov, especially his second piano concerto. If she heard a piece of music that she liked, but did not recognise, she could not rest until she found out what it was. One such case was the haunting piece used many years ago by the BBC (radio) to introduce the late night programme "Epilogue". She enquired and wrote letters until she discovered that it was Samuel Barber's *Adagio for Strings*. This remained especially dear to her, and we chose it for her funeral.

Around the house, Mum would often sing or whistle. She could do both very well – not just the classics, but the romantic songs from her young days in the 1930s. When Dad was in the Army, I was very familiar with her singing, wishing for his safe return, such songs as "This is my lovely day", "I'll see you again, whenever spring breaks through again", and especially

"We'll gather lilacs in the spring again".

As the years went by and television entered their lives, Jim and Lenna enjoyed relaxing with their favourite programmes, which ranged from the News and sport, to drama, documentaries and travel programmes. A special treat was to watch the annual Leeds international piano competition.

By this time they had moved to a larger house in the same road. It was not until they retired from business that Lenna was able to make a start on fulfilling personal ambitions she had held since she was a schoolgirl. All her life, she had wanted to write a book and paint pictures. Art and literature meant a great deal to her, but without the means, encouragement or confidence to undertake any formal training, she had not been able to do anything but appreciate the work of others.

Her great love was the work of the Impressionists. She read the artists' lives, bought cards and prints of their paintings and saw exhibitions in Manchester whenever possible.

Somehow, at sixty-nine, Lenna made a start. She went to an evening class at the local school and began to paint in oils. This became an absorbing interest, and her paintings are a lasting memory for us. They are small, detailed and evocative landscapes of her beloved Bluebell Wood; the scenery of the Yorkshire Dales (my home for thirty years); and of the Lake District and Scotland where she latterly took holidays, with Vivien and family or myself.

Vivien and I grew up and have led our own lives, while retaining close family ties. I became a teacher and local historian and settled in Wensleydale in 1970. I married David Hall, also an historian, who died in 1990. Vivien stayed in Rudheath, married twice and has three children, Lorna, Jamie and Stuart. Lenna and Jim greatly enjoyed the cheerful company of their grandchildren. Vivien and Peter cared for Mum and Dad in their old age, and enabled them to maintain as much independence as possible. They took them shopping, to football matches and on holiday, besides providing company and doing a thousand and one little jobs. Mum still rode her bicycle until a few weeks before she died. She had suffered from osteo-arthritis since she was in her forties and found cycling easier than walking to the local shops

Lenna's best-known achievement was the writing of her own memories, which she completed in about 1982. It sat, in typescript, on the reference shelf in Northwich Library, until it was published by Léonie Press in 1996 as *Memories of a Cheshire Childhood*. Dad was very proud of her work, but he died a few weeks before her book was launched. For twenty years he had suffered from emphysema, but he never lost his quiet optimism. He remained cheerful and positive, in spite of many setbacks in health and circumstance.

I have mentioned the wedding anniversary present of 1950, but it was not a "one-off" gift. Every year, without fail, Lenna and Jim exchanged anniversary cards, with affectionate greetings, and Jim always arranged for a dozen red roses to appear on 21 June.

When Dad died, Mum was devastated. They had been married for fifty-nine years, had cared for and helped each other, and looked for nothing more from life than to be together. Mum's loneliness was unbearable. Vivien and her family lived nearby and cared for her in every way. They were able to take her on holiday to France, in her last summer, something she had always wanted to do. She lived to see her great-grandson, Jostein (Stuart's son), and was able to visit him in Norway. She loved his company and was delighted to have him to stay.

However, her sadness defeated her. After three years without Jim, she suffered several heart attacks and died in hospital on 14 November 1999, shortly before her eighty-fifth birthday. She died of a broken heart.

A Final Tribute

Lenna's grand-daughter, Lorna, wrote the following moving tribute which she read at the funeral on November 14, 1999:

As the eldest of the grandchildren, we thought it fitting that I should say a few words on behalf of us all.

We should not view today as a sad day, it is a tribute; a celebration of a wonderful life fully lived.

Let's remember Lenna, not with sadness, but with happiness for the rich and varied life that she had and of the legacy that she has left. Two wonderful daughters, three happy healthy grandchildren and a beautiful great-grandson, not to mention a recollection of her childhood memories which has captured the imagination of people, not just here, but on the other side of the world. She was also a brilliant artist as you can see by her work here.

But not least of all, she left us with a wealth of happy memories, memories which will always be with us to treasure.

It was Lenna's wish for several years that she could be with Grandpa. She was very good at expressing her thoughts on paper and a few days ago we found a notebook where she had written, "if God will let us be together in love as we used to be, I will be happy forever."

It's our belief that her prayer has been answered.

MEMORIES
OF A CHESHIRE
CHILDHOOD

by Lenna
Bickerton

Lenna Bickerton spent her early years during the First World War living with her grandparents in the close-knit community of Lostock Gralam. Her mother, a young war widow, worked in an ammunition factory at Wincham and afterwards in domestic service in Manchester, travelling home on the Sunday afternoon "dripping train" to see her daughter.

When Lenna's mother married again, the small family eventually moved into one of the first council houses to be built at Rudheath – a piece of good fortune they regarded as little short of a miracle. Lenna lived on the same estate until she died.

In her book Lenna describes life in those far-off days through the sharp senses of a child. Her memories are vivid: duck eggs for breakfast, dancing to Grandad's gramophone, a near-tragedy at Hesketh's watermill, her schooldays, the sights and sounds of old Northwich, the smells of wild flowers, busy boat traffic on the Trent and Mersey Canal – and the menacing 'Ginny Greenteeth'.

The young Lenna roamed the fields, woods and flashes around Lostock Gralam and Rudheath in a carefree way any modern child would envy. She said: "Boredom was a word we never used in our childhood. Our imagination came into play to make up for the lack of material things and, most of all, we had freedom to wander at will in the countryside."

Price: £4.99
Postage: £1.00

ISBN 1 901253 00 7

Other books published by the Léonie Press, an imprint of Anne Loader Publications, 13 Vale Road, Hartford, Northwich, Cheshire CW8 1PL, Gt Britain, include:

A House with Sprit: A dedication to Marbury Hall by Jackie Hamlett and Christine Hamlett (ISBN 1 901253 01 5), price £8.99

Ulu Tiram: A cameo of life in Malaya at the time of 'The Emergency' by Peter and Kathleen Thomas (ISBN 1 901253 05 8), price £5.75

A Bull by the Back Door: How an English family find their own paradise in rural France by Anne Loader
(ISBN 1 901253 06 6), price £8.99

The Way We Were: Omnibus edition of Les Cooper's Crewe memories 'Over My Shoulder' and 'Another's War'
by Les Cooper (ISBN 1 901253 07 4), price £7.99

A Nun's Grave: A Novel set in the Vale Royal of England
by Alan K Leicester (ISBN 1 901253 08 5) price £7.99

The Duck with a Dirty Laugh: More family adventures in rural France
by Anne Loader (ISBN 1 901253 09 0), price £8.99

Nellie's Story - A Life of Service
by Elizabeth Ellen Osborne (ISBN 1 901253 09 0), price £5.99

Diesel Taff: From 'The Barracks' to Tripoli
by Austin Hughes (ISBN 1 90125314 7), price £8.99

Woollyback
by Alan Fleet (ISBN 1 901253 18 X), price £8.99

A Whiff of Fresh Air (plus CD)
by Margaret Dignum (ISBN 1 901253 20 1), price £9.99

Two Birds and No Stones: It's a short life – fill it!
by Geoffrey Morris (ISBN 1 901250 17 1), price £8.99